Homes Fit For Heroes

The aftermath of the First World War
1918-1939

Trevor Yorke

Foreword by Frank Field MP

COUNTRYSIDE BOOKS
NEWBURY BERKSHIRE

COUNTRYSIDE BOOKS
3 Catherine Road
Newbury, Berkshire

To view our complete range of books,
please visit us at
www.countrysidebooks.co.uk

ISBN 978 1 84674 3498

Illustrations and modern photographs by Trevor Yorke

Produced through The Letterworks Ltd., Reading
Typeset by KT Designs, St Helens
Printed by The Holywell Press, Oxford

Contents

Foreword

This is a most wonderful book and I say so on a number of fronts.

It is a fitting follow-up to Trevor Yorke's previous volume *The Trench*. That was a fine work and *Homes Fit for Heroes* builds on it.

The book is beautifully illustrated. It is doubtful whether anyone has brought together a better collection of photographs illustrating the story of those who attempted to build a new world, and the sheer range of buildings they constructed, to build a land fit for heroes.

The text, of course, is crucial. Here we have a concise story from the outbreak of the First World War to the war clouds breaking over our heads again in 1939. Lloyd George is one, if not the, political hero of the author. It is difficult now to imagine the sheer drive of the man and how short a time he had to build a winning coalition from late 1916 to 1918.

Lloyd George's huge energy then went on a social reform programme, much of which was not fulfilled. One area that was fulfilled was his wish to transform the housing conditions of the working class – despite the label that hangs round his neck that there was no land fit for heroes.

Quickly Lloyd George established a committee under John Tudor Walters to come up with a plan that could provide beautiful, yes, beautiful, housing for working people which they could afford. The Tudor Walters report, as Trevor notes, published in November 1918, was so influential that it set the standard for much of the housebuilding in Britain right up until the 1960s.

I would draw two main political

Frank Field MP

lessons from this text. The first would be about idealism. For whatever reason Lloyd George managed to act as a lightning rod for a growing demand in the country in the number and quality of houses that should be provided for working people. The standards were way ahead of their time as this book makes plain. Many tried to dismiss these standards as being 'idealistic' but they would be proved wrong. The second lesson I draw is the important role of leadership. Lloyd George, who quickly became part of the establishment, also maintained a presence outside in the country. It was this person, the one that decided to make providing decent housing of beautiful quality for working class people a reality, who should take the main bow. But he was joined by another establishment figure, who never lost his roots in his community and worked as a doctor in the community, Addison, to carry the programme through in the very early stages. These two people used the power of the state to direct its protective power in a different direction and to deliver, initially in catering for a near universal demand for most working class people. We need that idealism and the ability to deliver in today's politics.

Some of the best illustrations in this book are of the range of estates that were built as a result of this initial drive from Lloyd George. As prime minister he also harnessed Dr Addison's enthusiasm as president of the Local Government Board which then carried all the Ministry of Health's responsibilities, including those for social housing. Addison, in 1919, converted Lloyd George's drive, and Tudor Walters' ideas, into legislative action in a great reforming act.

But I must not go on as I do not want to steal too much of the delight that will engage the reader of this glimpse of who planned the great future, who achieved so much, and how this was picked up by one of Addison's successors, Aneurin Bevan, as health minister once war was over.

Frank Field

Introduction

The First World War did not only initiate men and women throughout Britain into the unrelenting horrors which an industrialised war machine could unleash, but also had a marked effect on the home front during the conflict and would shape the nation in the decades which followed. Wars from earlier periods had been celebrated, with places named after famous battles and stories told of heroic acts, but for most people daily life had gone on as usual. This time it was different. The huge scale of the operation, the frightening new technology and the fact that millions of the men fighting were volunteers and conscripts, not professional soldiers, brought the war directly to the heart of the nation. The terrible loss of life which was felt in nearly every community across the British Isles would inspire people in authority to endeavour to ensure that those who survived would return to a better life. The key area upon which they would focus was the living conditions of the ordinary 'Tommy', and the 'Homes Fit For Heroes' which were created during the 1920s and 1930s will be the core subject of this book.

The story of these momentous changes in society begins with a brief look at social conditions before the war and at what life was like for those living and working at home during the war years. The following chapters explain why the building of new houses for the working classes was so important and how it was put into practice. They describe the revolutionary housing estates that were built and show why the new homes were such an improvement on what had gone before. More than that, this book also considers the problems of demobilising millions of men once the conflict ended, how those who did not return were remembered and why the war had such a dramatic impact upon all classes of society. In each chapter there are boxed-out pieces of extra information, describing for instance the people who were responsible for trying to build the new society, and some of the sources of information which can be used to help trace the history of family members who lived through these times of change.

The Trench: Life and Death on the Western Front 1914-1918, described the conditions soldiers had to endure in the First World War. *Homes Fit For Heroes* takes up the story once the guns had fallen silent. Using photos, drawings and contemporary documents this colourful illustrated guide shows what life was like for the returning soldiers and their families, and how for many the battle to survive would continue in peacetime. It outlines the importance of the post-war period in shaping our modern world and the buildings and memorials we can see all around us today. More than that I hope it will also inspire and empower readers to investigate the story of their own family once those who fought had returned from the horrors of the Western Front.

Trevor Yorke

www.trevoryorke.co.uk
Follow me on Facebook at
trevoryorke-author

My mother's father, George Lee, fought with the Royal Field Artillery during the First World War. He is pictured here in the centre of the front row with his legs crossed, alongside colleagues from his regiment. After serving in France, they were posted to the Middle East where George spent most of his service until he returned late in 1919.

1918 Armistice Day. Soldiers celebrating the end of the war. Despite the flag-waving that greeted Britain's returning troops many felt resentment for the leaders who had sent them to die. The concept of peace was also bewildering for many of them after years of conflict.

Britain During 1914-1918

Homes, Women and Air Raids

The Prime Minister, David Lloyd George, walked onto the stage at the Grand Theatre in Wolverhampton on 24 November 1918 to deliver a speech outlining his vision for post-war Britain. With the Armistice agreed less than two weeks earlier, heralding a suspension in hostilities (the First World War did not officially end until the Treaty of Versailles was signed in the following June) this victorious leader was already beginning his campaign for the forthcoming general election. His message that evening recognised the horrors which the returning soldiers had faced: 'I have been there at the door of the furnace and witnessed it, but that is not being in it, and I saw them march into the furnace.' At the same time though, he urged the audience to seize the opportunity which the Armistice presented: 'I want us to take advantage of this new spirit. Don't let us waste this victory merely in ringing joybells.'

Lloyd George was not just revelling in the moment but making a pledge to the nation that he could guide them to a better future. 'What is our task? To make Britain a fit country for heroes to live in.' In this memorable line he acknowledged that soldiers returning from the Western Front would expect a higher standard of living than before the war and that it would be the improvement of housing which would be at the centre of his plans.

Working class housing set back to back or tightly packed into rear courts as in this photo was seen as part of the reason for the poor health of many potential recruits for the First World War. Despite risking their lives for their country many soldiers coming back from the Western Front would be returning to unsanitary conditions like these.

Before exploring how he tried to achieve this and what life was actually like for the men and women who had fought in or supported the war effort, it is worth taking a moment to see why this was the key issue of the time and what the state of the nation was in 1918 as the war drew to a close.

The Nation's Housing

The century of industrial revolution, expanding trade and growing financial strength which preceded the First World War had turned Britain into a leading world power. It had seemed to those in authority that it was well equipped to fight a major European conflict. However, as the war drew on and volunteering turned into conscription so the relentless demand for fit young men on the Western Front exposed shortcomings in society. Underpinning those who had benefited from Britain's industrial success were millions who struggled to make ends meet, had poor diets and lived in slum conditions which directly affected their health. When their country called, many were simply not fit enough to join the army. Their rejection opened the eyes of government and army officials to the importance of this long festering problem. As the conflict drew to a close this issue, along with the fact that millions of soldiers would soon be returning with high expectations,

meant that improving the housing of the working classes became a hot topic. It would not just be a reward from a grateful nation but was also needed to put the population in a fit state for going forward.

David Lloyd George (1863-1945). This energetic Welshman (he was actually born in Manchester) was one of the most influential British leaders of the 20th century. As Chancellor of the Exchequer (1908-15) he was responsible for introducing state support of the sick and unemployed and then as Prime Minister (1916-22) he guided the country to victory in the First World War and helped shape the peace agreement. Lloyd George (his surname was George but he added Lloyd out of respect for his uncle) was key in driving forward new social reforms and was instrumental in the passing of the Housing and Town Planning Act 1919 which instigated the first large scale building of council houses.

The unsatisfactory state of working class housing had been known about by successive governments. Numerous reports over the previous 50 years had highlighted the issue for the working masses in the industrial towns and cities that had created the vast wealth of Britain and its Empire. However, the stern attitude of 'self help' which permeated Victorian society meant that central government and local authorities were reluctant to become involved in solving the problem. Private builders provided most of the housing in the rapidly expanding urban areas but in many places this was squeezed into narrow courts at the rear of existing buildings or crammed back to back in blocks which lacked running water and proper sanitation. Outbreaks of disease focused attention on the problem but it was usually only the personal involvement of benevolent individuals who led the way out of it. They created model housing estates for factory staff or blocks of flats and terraces with improved sanitation for working families which demonstrated the benefits gained by good housing. By the opening decade of the 20th century conditions for many had also been improved by rising wages and living standards which had enabled them to rent more spacious and modern terraced homes.

There were still millions, though, who were trapped in ageing and unhealthy slums and who did not have the income to escape. The only time most local authorities became involved was in providing new sanitary accommodation as part of the planned clearance of a slum area. They were permitted to raise rates to finance these schemes under the 1875 Artisans' Dwellings Act but its use tended to be limited

Glasgow Rent Strike 1915

As workers flooded into Glasgow to take jobs in the shipyards and factories the increase in demand for housing meant that many landlords seized the opportunity to raise rents. They thought the women, with their menfolk away at the Front, would be a soft touch and if they did not pay up the extra rent they were threatened with eviction. However the female tenants, who were already unified against the poor maintenance of their homes, quickly rose up to fight the demand for up to 25% increases. Led by Mary Barbour they refused to pay and would raise the alarm when a bailiff's officer was spied and pelt them with flour bombs and other projectiles until they fled. Around 20,000 tenants were on rent strike by late 1915 and the movement was spreading to other cities. The issue came to a head in November when there was an attempt to prosecute 18 tenants for non-payment, causing a huge peaceful demonstration which forced the authorities to contact Lloyd George directly. Within a month the Rent Restriction Act had been passed which fixed rents for the duration of the war at pre-1914 levels.

and small in scale. There were exceptions though. In Liverpool, for instance, a Conservative council was responsible for the building of an impressive number of new flats to house the working classes.

For those living in the countryside, where labourers' wages were usually lower than those of their urban counterparts, the situation was often worse. Paintings of rose-covered tumbledown cottages which so romanticised the countryside for urban Victorians longing to escape their dirty industrial surroundings inavertently recorded the terrible state of labourers' housing in many areas of the country. Health inspectors in some regions found children sleeping on wet bedding due to gaping holes in the roof above, over ten people crammed into a single bedroom and families sick with fever as they had to share a room with a corpse. Agricultural depression in some sectors of the industry during the closing decades of the 19th century had only heightened the problem for many rural families, creating similar health issues to those which restricted the conscription of fit men during the war.

The key problem for both urban and rural working families was that the rent for better housing was too high (90% of householders were tenants when the war started in 1914). The cost of erecting the buildings and the return the landlords expected put improved housing out of the reach of many families. Terraces were often built just a few at a time by small-scale private builders and as they were buying bricks, timber and fittings in small quantities the material costs were high. Few attempted to simplify the design and construction of housing in order to lower costs. There had been some experiments with concrete houses and competitions had been held to design homes which would be cheaper to build to try and reduce rents but this had had little effect on the mass housing market by the time war broke out in 1914. If Lloyd George and his coalition government, who were victorious in the general election in December 1918, were going to make a difference they would have to try and solve these issues and on an unprecedented scale.

Railways, Coal and Munitions

At the same time as tackling the housing crisis the new government would have to turn the country away from a war footing. Industry was geared up to support the armed services and the country at the end of 1918 was in no fit state to try to reclaim its position in world markets. In addition, life for many had changed beyond recognition, both at work and at home.

The railways, at the time divided up into numerous individual companies, were taken over by the government at the outbreak of war and control passed to a Railway Executive Committee. This planned move enabled over 100,000 soldiers and their horses, vehicles and tons of supplies to be moved to coastal ports in the first month of the conflict. The system had to cope with increased traffic and a shift in its normal patterns of delivery as raw materials, workers and soldiers needed to be transported to military establishments and ports. This strain on the railway network and its staff had resulted in accidents. The worst on the British railways occurred at Quintinshill, near Gretna Green in May 1915 where 227 people, mainly soldiers, lost their lives.

Coal was essential not only to power the nation's factories and heat its homes but also as the fuel for its navy and railways. However in the first year of the war nearly a quarter of all miners left the industry to take up arms, attracted by the regular pay and an escape from the horrendous conditions in the pits. Coal was also in high demand through the increased traffic on the railways so the government had to quickly step in to stop more of them leaving. The inevitable coal shortages as supplies were prioritised for the war effort resulted in queuing and rationing at home and prosecutions for those caught stealing it. When the war was drawing to a close it was the miners who were first called back and rationing continued long after the Armistice had been signed.

HM Factory, Gretna was built in the wake of the 1915 munitions shortage and could manufacture 800 tons of cordite a week. To house the sudden influx of thousands of workers from Ireland and around the Empire two townships were created at Gretna and Eastrigg. Sir Raymond Unwin, who had worked on Letchworth Garden City and workers' housing projects before the war, helped to design the timber and brick housing you can see in this photo. The street names reflected the diverse ethnic mix with Melbourne Avenue, Delhi Road and Vancouver Drive still surviving today. The factory was promptly shut after the war but parts of the site continued in military use with the history of the site now recorded at the Devil's Porridge Museum in Eastrigg (a name coined by Sir Arthur Conan Doyle in 1917 when describing the mix of nitroglycerin and gun cotton that was being produced here).

At the outbreak of hostilities the military leaders had anticipated a mobile war so when the western front became static and entrenched many of the types of weapon they had stockpiled were found not to be suitable for the new form of warfare which quickly evolved. This resulted in a munitions shortage, especially of high explosive shells, and a Ministry of Munitions was formed in May 1915 with David Lloyd George charged with resolving the problem. New factories were built but as it would be some time before they could be properly up and running railway workshops, which made parts for rolling stock, were used to fill the gap. They continued to make munitions throughout the war. Before 1914 Britain was producing around 50,000 shells a year but this increased to over 50 million during the war, in addition to 26,000 big guns and 250,000 machine guns.

Because of the importance of wartime production those employed were in a strong bargaining position, though patriotic feeling limited their desire to complain about certain aspects of their work. The Munitions Act 1915 forbade strike action in this vital wartime industry but also protected workers, setting maximum hours, fixing wages and providing for improved conditions. Despite this, trade union membership nearly doubled during the war and the unions themselves became better funded and organised. There were strikes, especially in the later years of the war, when wages failed to keep up with rising inflation and fatigue from working long hours built up. When the country went to the polls in 1918 the trade unions were in an influential position and funded Labour candidates, with the party gaining 57 MPs – within six years the Labour Party would form their first government.

Women at Work

Much of the increased production in support of the war effort was only possible because women were willing and able to take over roles formerly performed by the men who had left for the Western Front. Despite prejudice from many in industry and agriculture an additional million and a half women were employed during the war, many in tasks which had formerly been considered as a male preserve.

The most notable contribution came in munitions factories. The majority of these 'munitionettes' worked in the production of shells, cartridges and bullets, so that by 1917 over 80% were being produced by women. Many employers were reluctant at first to employ women until pressure was applied by the Ministry of Munitions, though few complained that they only had to pay them around half the wage of their male counterparts. Serious health hazards also arose through the long term contact with chemicals, especially trinitrotoluene (TNT) which not only affected organs and fertility but also turned the skin a yellow or orange colour, gaining those who worked with it the nickname 'Canary Girls'.

The Women's Land Army was formed in January 1917 when German U-boats targeting British food supply ships created an urgent need for more hands to turn land over to food

Around 700,000 women were employed in munitions factories during the war. In addition there were many more in other formerly male roles including over 70,000 who helped keep the railways running, 160,000 in the civil service and Post Office, while the number in finance and banking rose sixfold and ten times as many women as normal worked in the utilities.

production. Around 15,000 girls from diverse backgrounds became farm hands during the war and made a vital contribution to keeping the nation fed during a time of severe shortages.

Although women were banned from the fighting in the trenches they also contributed to the war effort both at home and abroad. Around 80,000 women signed up for Queen Mary's Auxiliary Army Corps (QMAAC), and played an active part in support

Many farmers found the idea of women in breeches working the land fanciful but others appreciated the help of the Women's Land Army in looking after livestock, working in the fields, and carrying out tasks which were formerly only performed by men.

of the Army, mainly in clerical, communications, cooking and transport roles. In March 1917 this became the Women's Army Auxiliary Corp. In the same year the Women's Royal Naval Service, better known as the Wrens, was formed with women taking similar roles to free up more men for active service, and in April 1918 the Women's Royal Air Force came into being. In addition to this at least 40,000 women enrolled at the start of the war in the Voluntary Aid Detachments and served in auxiliary hospitals and in support of military staff on the Western Front, where female nursing and medical staff played a prominent part.

Bombing Raids

The strategy of terrorising a city and taking out vital industries and transport links by bombing from aircraft was an idea spawned in the First rather than the Second World War. For the first time civilians could be threatened in their own homes on British soil. Bombing raids were first conducted with Zeppelins from 1915 but they were not that effective, especially after defences improved with searchlights, guns and planes armed with incendiary bullets which could set the airships alight. However from 1917 the Germans began using Gotha aircraft and bombs above 300kg (by 1918 1,000kg) in

Soldiers who were seriously wounded in action were quickly patched up on the Western Front and then dispatched back to Britain via ship and ambulance trains. Here they would have surgery and recuperate in either the main hospitals under the War Office and Admiralty or in one of the dependant auxiliary units which were run by volunteers. By the end of the war there were over 1,400 of these auxiliary hospitals established in country houses, schools or large public buildings. There were many jobs in a hospital which were traditionally male but two suffragists, Doctors Flora Murray and Louisa Garrett Anderson founded a military hospital in Endell Street, London which was run entirely by women. Despite stiff opposition from some quarters it ran for five years and cared for 26,000 patients, with staff often working late into the night when the ambulance trains arrived. The auxiliary hospital in this photo was exclusively for officers and was established in Pembroke Lodge, Kensington, the residence of Andrew Bonar Law. He would become Britain's shortest serving Prime Minister in 1922.

Munitions Factories

The most dangerous aspect of munitions factory work was the risk of igniting the explosives. There were numerous incidents and a number of catastrophic explosions. Faversham had been the site of gunpowder manufacture since the 16th century and a huge 500 acre factory built during the war at nearby Uplees was a major centre for high explosive production and the filling of bombs and shells. On 2 April 1916 a fire caused 200 tonnes of TNT to ignite, the blast killing 115 men and boys. As it was a Sunday there were no women working in the plant at the time. A huge blast on 19 January 1917 destroyed part of the factory in Silvertown in East London when a fire ignited 50 tonnes of TNT; 73 were killed and over 400 injured. The death toll would have been far worse if it had been at a busy time of day. At a National Shell Filling Factory in Chilwell, Notts only 8 tonnes of the lethal explosive ignited on 1 July 1918 but 134 lost their lives with only 32 of the bodies recovered being identifiable.

total air raids claimed the lives of around 1,400 people and wounded over 3,400 others, but overall they failed to make a notable impression on the British war effort.

Life at home

Home life was very much affected as the war dragged on. The price of many essential products doubled, queueing outside shops became a daily chore and a shortage of domestic help meant that even the well off had to fend for themselves. Rising rents caused hardships for many families and there were rent strikes in some cities until the government introduced controls.

As British ships were sunk by submarine or blockaded from ports across Europe so certain essential foods became short on supply. The

weight. These more effective raids were mainly targeted at London and a series of balloons with steel wires stretched between them plus a defensive force of around 200 aircraft were employed to keep the Gothas at bay. Twenty eight people died when a printing works which was being used as an air raid shelter was destroyed on 28 January 1918 and 20 were killed, including soldiers on leave, when one bomb hit St Pancras station in the following month. In

The Imperial War Museum, London was founded in March 1917 with the intention of recording the experiences of those at home as well as in the firing line during the First World War. Adverts were put in ration books encouraging people to donate memorabilia as well as military hardware and the museum today has over 10 million items and collections. It was originally opened at Crystal Palace in 1920 but after a time here and at South Kensington the museum was relocated to its current site in 1936 in part of the former Bethlem Royal Hospital at Southwark.

At Warrington Avenue, Maida Vale, London a complete row of houses was flattened on 7 March 1918 by the largest German bomb to fall in Britain during the war. It claimed the lives of ten people and caused damage to hundreds of properties in the area. The top photo shows the scene of devastation the day after. The bottom photo is of the exact spot today with the Arts and Crafts style replacement houses built in the 1920s standing out from the tall terraces either side.

government took action before the situation escalated and introduced rationing in January 1918. Only set amounts of meat, sugar, cheese, butter, milk and flour could be purchased with ration cards. Even King George V and Queen Mary were issued with them. Shortages continued after hostilities ended and butter was still rationed in 1920. Families were also encouraged to grow their own food and public areas were turned over to allotments. These actions helped to stave off the rioting and revolution witnessed elsewhere across Europe in the closing years of the war.

So, it was into this situation of instability that the millions of soldiers returning from the Western Front would have to be integrated. The first issue for the government to deal with was how to practically get a huge army and all its supplies back across the Channel and home.

Chapter 2

A Return to Normality

Demobilisation 1918-1919

The speed with which Germany's position deteriorated from one of near victory in the spring of 1918 to the verge of collapse six months later caught many by surprise. The British government was aware of their precarious state in October but this news was not widely broadcast so as to avoid a slackening off of the war effort. The signing of the Armistice on 11 November 1918 came as a sudden and welcome relief to most, although some in the munitions industry feared for their jobs with this unexpected news.

Now the authorities had to quickly put into action their plans to transport home from the Western Front millions of men, animals and vehicles, tons of munitions, and other military hardware that would no longer be needed by the standing army which would remain in Europe. This would involve chartering ships for the crossing of the Channel, organising ports to receive them, arranging for trains to carry men and equipment around the country, establishing dispersal stations for the demobilisation of soldiers, collecting arms and ammunition, selling off surplus stores and equipment, and organising the mountain of forms and certificates associated with the process. In addition there were the thousands of wounded men to cater for, soldiers from the dominions who would need shipping home and

Royal Field Artillery gunners landing at Dover on their way to be demobilised and return home.

19

enemy prisoners of war to be returned to their own country. And then there was the workforce at home which had laboured the past four years in support of the armed forces and who would now either have to return to their former roles or lose their job.

The greatest fear for the authorities was that of revolution, as had erupted in Russia only the year before. A mass of worn out, disgruntled soldiers returning to a country with no guaranteed employment and poor housing could spark a socialist rising. The government would therefore not only have to solve the physical issue of demobilisation but also perform it in a controlled manner so the great influx of returning soldiers would not overwhelm the system, and at the same time give them hope for a brighter future so they knew their sacrifices had not been in vain.

Demobilisation problems

The plan centred upon getting industry back on a commercial footing at the earliest opportunity. Many factories had been converted to wartime production and would need switching back, while the companies would want their key employees back on the job at the earliest opportunity. In other countries, like France, soldiers were to be returned home dependent on their age, with the oldest first and youngest last.

After their arrival at port most soldiers' next stop was at a major railway station before heading to a camp for demobilisation. Pictured here are Grenadier Guards arriving at St Pancras Station, London (top) and the 4th Royal Scots marching out of Waverley Station, Edinburgh (bottom).

In Britain it was decided to enforce a more complicated system which would give priority to those who had key roles or skills in certain trades or worked for companies which were ready to offer them immediate employment. Industry was to be fed and not flooded, although with the coal shortages miners had been rushed home and some had returned even before the Armistice was signed.

The first step had already been taken with an order on 21 October 1918 for soldiers to record their industrial group (from a list of 43), their precise trade, physical condition and marital status in their Army Service and Pay Book (Army Book

The process of demobilisation for the individual soldier involved completion of a number of forms and certificates which if they can be found today give a brief glimpse into the lives of our gallant predecessors. Their journey from the conflict zone brought most back to transit camps at Calais, Dunkirk, Le Havre or Dieppe while they awaited the crossing to Britain. They would land at ports along the south and east coast from Weymouth round to Harwich where they would be transported by train to the dispersal station or camp nearest to their home destination. The main dispersal stations were at Kinross, Duddingston (Edinburgh) and Georgetown (Glasgow) for Scotland. In England they were at Ripon (North Yorks), Harrowby (near Grantham, Lincs), Heaton Park (Manchester), Clipstone (near Mansfield, Notts), Chiseldon (near Swindon, Wilts), Fovant (near Salisbury, Wilts), Thetford (Norfolk), Shorncliffe (Folkestone), Purfleet (Essex) and Wimbledon (London) although this latter was replaced by a larger station at Crystal Palace in January 1919. Park Hall (Oswestry) covered most of Wales. The country was divided up into groups of counties with a number and letter code which would indicate which of these stations or the smaller camps they were dispersed at. Some found the stations in chaos and faced a long wait while others discovered an efficient team with those in charge priding themselves on their ability to process thousands of men each day.

The soldiers would be expected to bring with them their uniform, gun, kit, boots and long greycoat, of which they were permitted to keep one uniform, one pair of boots, their underclothing and a small kit. They would also receive a suit of plain clothes or an allowance of 52s 6d instead. The government had arranged for each soldier and officer to have an Out of Work Donation Policy which would permit them to receive up to 26 weeks' unemployment pay within the first year after demobilisation. Soldiers and officers also received a Protection Certificate which would be used to claim their final three wage payments during the 28 days of furlough (leave) which would begin immediately after demobilisation. Finally they were given a warrant for a single rail ticket and could return home in uniform with their steel helmet and greycoat (their greycoats had to be returned to a local railway station within their furlough period, although some were in such a poor state they did not bother to keep them). Those who were not remaining in active service were discharged to Class Z Army Reserve which meant they could still be called up if the nation was in dire need.

1918-1919 Flu Pandemic

The closing months of the war and the subsequent demobilisation of troops was taking place during the worst outbreak of influenza in modern times. Its impact was even more tragic as unusually this flu virus proved deadly to all age groups. Many of the soldiers who had survived enemy fire and disease in the trenches were to be fatally struck down while waiting in camps in France or during their return home.

The virus spread rapidly across Britain during late 1918 and early 1919 and despite actions being taken like spraying chemicals in the streets it claimed the lives of 228,000. It also spread around the world with devastating effect. In India where many of their doctors were away serving with the Allies in Europe this flu outbreak killed around 16 million, more people than died from all sides fighting during the four years of the First World War. In total it is likely that close to 50 million people died globally.

The first recorded cases were in American army camps in March 1918 but this was a milder, less fatal form. It soon spread through all armies fighting in the Western Front but as they had news blackouts of stories which could lower morale the outbreak was hushed up. The exception was in neutral Spain where it was made public, especially after the King contracted it, with the effect that soldiers assumed it had originated there and hence called it 'Spanish Flu'. It could strike people down in a matter of days, with exceptional reports stating that someone who had seemed fit and well at breakfast could be dead by tea.

64). The next stage was for them to fill in a Civil Employment Form on which they would record their age, condition, former employer and if they had received a definite offer of work upon their return. At the same time employers in Britain had to return application forms to list those who they needed back as a priority because they had key roles or could help in organising other workers. This information was processed during November 1918 and final lists of the priority men were sent out in early December to commanding officers who could then make out a dispersal draft (only 3% of each draft could contain officers themselves). Those in command did have a certain flexibility in also returning men who had long or expired service, but in most cases the draft would list the men on their ability to contribute to industry rather than their past sacrifices to the nation.

This complicated plan soon ran into trouble as army chiefs allowed others not on the industry list to be demobilised early. In addition to this men who were already back in Britain because they were on leave pointed out there was little point in sending them back abroad only to be returned home again. If they were in a special industry and had a definite offer of work then these 'contract men' were allowed to be demobilised early. There were further delays because of bad winter weather and the problems of getting transport across the Channel. By Christmas 1918 eleven dispersal stations were up and running around Britain, and approximately 10,000 soldiers returning from France and 1,000 contract men were being demobilised every day.

Compared with other nations like America this rate of progress was seen as slow, not only by the soldiers gathering in the French coastal ports expecting a prompt return but also by employers still waiting to get their key staff back. Frustration grew amongst many of the men, especially those who realised that they faced a

Troops queuing up to exchange their foreign currency at a London railway terminus before going to their demobilisation camps.

Soldiers queuing up to receive unemployment policies (top left), hand in their guns (top right), be measured for their civilian suits (bottom left) and finally leaving the demobilisation camp for the railway station and home (bottom right).

Demobilisation Forms

The following are the main army forms used by soldiers and officers during the process of demobilisation:

Z1: Certificate of Demobilisation.

Z3: Officer's Protection Certificate.

Z7: Claim form for Repatriation to an Overseas British Possession or a Foreign Country.

Z11: Protection Certificate and Certificate of Identity: recorded his details, where he had served. It was also used for stamps for receiving pay during the final 28 days, getting a ticket for the final journey home and when claiming unemployment benefit.

Z12: Protection Certificate.

Z18: Certificate of Employment: this was issued to record a soldier's role or roles during the war and to assist him in getting employment afterwards.

Z22: Statement as to Disability: every soldier and officer had to fill this in to establish whether they intended to make a claim for disability due to military service or not. If they did they had to fill in details in the lower half of the form. If left blank it only meant they were not claiming and not that they had suffered no injury.

Z44: Plain Clothes Allowance.

Z50: Returned Greycoat form: they received £1 from a railway station upon its return within 28 days of demobilisation.

were violent outbreaks, marches and demonstrations as men grew tired of waiting. The new Secretary of State for War, Winston Churchill, acted in January 1919 by abandoning the industrial plan and started to bring back the men dependent upon their length of service and the number of wounds they had received. There was a priority for the older men first so 18 year olds who had signed up in 1918 were now going to be the last to be demobilised. This system seemed fairer to most and the higher pay offered to those who had to wait helped dissolve discontent.

There was a further problem when it was realised that a larger standing army would be required than at first thought. It was needed to maintain peace in Europe and the Middle East as it was not known how the Germans would react to the peace treaty when the terms were made known. The British Army were also involved in the troubles in Russia, India and Ireland. Hence many men were to remain in service to provide the British contribution of 900,000 men to the post-war army. The list of who would be required was posted on 30 January 1919. The tens of thousands of women who had supported the war effort in the Women's Army Auxiliary Corp were often amongst the last to come home as many were required for clerical work as

long wait because their trade was not essential and despite their long service in the army. There was also resentment towards the contract men who were going home to their loved ones just because of the luck of being on leave at the time. This anger boiled over in many of the camps and there

There had been trouble during the latter stages of the war, with over 600 soldiers court-martialled and sentenced to death for acts of sedition and mutiny in 1918. In January 1919 soldiers in Calais and other French ports seized control of their camps in protest at the poor conditions and treatment by superiors. Around 10,000 soldiers at the Folkestone garrison protested too and around 7,000 marched into Brighton from Shoreham Camp to complain about the delay in demobilisation. Canadian soldiers fed up with the wait demonstrated their frustration at their camp in Rhyl in March and the situation was only suppressed when a number of soldiers were killed. The soldiers pictured here were 'Leave Men' marching to Whitehall to protest at being sent back overseas.

part of the demobilisation process. The return of those who had served from Britain's colonial countries was determined by the availability of space on shipping although if they had signed up after the start of the war their transit was paid for. Their demobilisation would take place in their home country once they had returned.

The new system resulted in more than 40,000 men being demobilised daily, such that by early February one million soldiers and officers had been demobilised and by the end of March it had risen to over two million. The British Army which had numbered nearly four million at the time of the Armistice was within a year down to around 900,000 and then was reduced to less than 250,000 by 1922.

The return and treatment of the wounded

The war had revolutionised medicine and the care of the wounded. The scale of the operation to treat men so they could return to the front line was vast as around 30% of soldiers were wounded at some point, with the figure closer to 60% in France. From the doctors, nurses, stretcher bearers and ambulance drivers of the Royal Army Medical Corps who risked their lives in the field to the volunteers who helped run auxiliary hospitals back home, there was a steep learning curve as the unprecedented numbers of injured came flooding in with horrific wounds inflicted by ever more powerful and lethal arms or with less understood injuries for which treatment was experimental. In addition there was the system

Amputees learning how to write with new artificial arms (top) and demonstrating using an axe in front of the King (bottom). The design of artificial limbs was transformed during the war from heavy, inflexible wooden types to far more functional aluminium devices as seen here. Despite these advances many soldiers though still preferred to use crutches.

required to provide medical supplies, from new technology like portable x-ray machines to the 300,000 pairs of glasses and 14,000 glass eyes supplied by the Army Spectacle Depot after it was established in 1916. The number of beds in military hospitals in Britain alone during the war grew from around 7,000 to more than 350,000.

The journey back to demobilisation for the casualties varied depending upon the nature and severity of their wounds or illness but their integration back into civilian life afterwards could be far more problematic. Over 300,000 men had suffered serious injury to their limbs during the war and around 41,000 had at least one arm or leg amputated. The process of amputation was crude and although attempts were made to improve methods it still left soldiers in great pain and trauma long after the removal. Special hospitals had been set up during the war including those at Shepherds Bush, London and Alder Hey, Liverpool which provided care for those with injured limbs and had rooms for electrical nerve treatment, gymnasiums, baths and massage departments and physiotherapy workshops in order to try and restore function after surgery. In addition there were special units like the one at Queen Mary's Hospital, Roehampton, London for amputees where they

The Luton Peace Day Riots
To celebrate the signing of the peace treaty with Germany at Versailles on 28 June 1919, a national holiday in Britain with a victory parade through London was planned for 19 July. Fifteen thousand troops marched through the capital with their route ending at a temporary wood and plaster Cenotaph erected in Whitehall. There were also various other events held around the country including a celebratory dinner in Luton, organised by the Mayor of this prosperous Bedfordshire town. Unfortunately this suspected war profiteer had angered ex-servicemen by refusing them permission for their own event, had banned women from his dinner and then made excessive charges so most soldiers could not afford to attend. This ignited a series of riots and attacks on property by the angry crowd which culminated in the burning down of the town hall. It was not until 1936 that the new town hall, pictured here with its steel frame clad in Portland stone, was opened. Its Neo Classical style was a modern interpretation of Classical architecture which was popular for public and commercial buildings in the 1920s and early 1930s.

could have artificial limbs fitted and training for a return to employment. Despite this the demand for artificial limbs outstripped supply and many were rushed through these hospitals without proper training. The situation was only brought under control after the Armistice stopped the influx of wounded although it also quickly brought about the closure of many of the hospitals and left amputees to fend for themselves.

For those who suffered injuries which left no physical scar the methods of treatment during the war were more experimental. Abnormal mental states (psychosis) and nervous diseases (neuroses) which were often termed as shell shock early in the war were known about from previous conflicts but were little understood at the time. Patients at first were treated in general hospitals before specialist neurological units were established, some doctors preferring to use counselling, others trying a more regimented system which could even include electric shock treatment.

Soldiers who suffered from these serious wounds were entitled to a war pension but it was graded upon

Ex-servicemen queuing up outside a labour exchange in 1919.

who had worked for the war effort at home but would now lose their jobs might tip the balance towards social unrest and revolution. The Minister of Labour in 1919, Robert Horne, stated that the government 'was faced with the immediate prospect of great masses of work people being thrown out on the streets without any means of livelihood'. The demand for gun ammunition stopped almost immediately after the armistice was signed and although many of the approximate three million employed in the industry were kept busy dealing with the existing stocks and armaments returned from the front some, especially women, found themselves quickly discarded.

the severity of their wounds. Those who had lost two limbs received the full pension but those who had lost one leg below the knee only received half. There were some employees who welcomed the war wounded into their factories but a large proportion of them found it hard to get work despite training. Now they had financial worries as well as dealing with their own physical strife. Many in society were also uncomfortable with those who bore physical reminders of the war or suffered from neurological problems. None of these wounded soldiers were invited to the Victory Parade on Peace Day in June 1919 and at that time the future for many of them must have seemed bleak.

Resettlement of war workers

Whilst trying to manage and appease the soldiers returning from the conflict zones, there were concerns that those

Horses which had served in the war in their thousands were either left behind in France and Belgium or brought back and usually sold off. At the auction pictured here in Romsey, Hants around 25,000 animals were sold in only three months.

Industry was trying to realign itself to pre-war production and the disruption and mass of returning soldiers only added to workers' discontent with millions going on strike in 1919, even more than in Germany, worried about their jobs, pay and the difficulty in getting housing. Some incidents, especially in sea ports, were directed towards minority ethnic workers, with anger vented at Afro-Caribbean, Chinese, African, Arab and Indian sailors who many thought were taking their jobs. In Cardiff during June 1919 mobs of British and Australian ex-servicemen terrorised the black community, killing three and injuring many others.

The government tried to keep workers busy in their own factories, but even at the Woolwich Arsenal the numbers employed dropped from 63,000 at the signing of the Armistice to around 24,000 in May 1919. Of these the number of women fell from 16,000 to only 2,700 over the same period and they usually fared even worse in the private sector. The government actively encouraged married women or those who were intending to marry to leave industry all together. Most others were expected to return to their previous roles, mainly in domestic service, with training offered for a select few in jobs which had been regarded as female before the war. However, work in the factories during the war had been better paid, the facilities provided were good and the strong comradeship and social life made many women understandably reluctant to return to the drudgery of domestic service and similar roles.

To help all workers a temporary act held wages up for six months while some were insured from unemployment through their trade union membership and from contributory benefit under Lloyd George's 1911 National Insurance Act. For those who were left looking for employment after the armistice the government introduced the Out of Work Donation. It was a benefit similar to that for returning soldiers but could only be drawn for a maximum period of 13 weeks in the six months after the armistice. It was a weekly payment of between 20 shillings for a single woman to around 36 shillings a week for a man with three children. Claims that the scheme was over generous and encouraging people to stop looking for work resulted in the cutting back of the sums paid in February 1919 but by May that year around 450,000 women and 220,000 men were still drawing the donation. Added to this were the returning soldiers who did not have guaranteed employment. The 31,000 who were claiming the Out of Work Donation in January

The conditions many soldiers had to endure on their journey back to Britain for demobilisation could be appalling. Robert Clough, MP for Keighley, Yorkshire, raised the issue in Parliament, citing the case of 'Private Hartley Hogarth, No. 025831, Royal Army Medical Corps, of Riddlesden, Keighley, who arrived home on the 21st February, 1919, travelled from Egypt to Italy, where the weather was very cold and snowy; that he was given two damp blankets and, along with other soldiers, made the journey to Le Havre, which occupied seven days and seven nights, in cattle trucks; that these men were then placed in tents in the pitch dark during heavy rain; that next morning they were marched six or seven miles, fully equipped, into Havre, where they were stripped and bathed, afterwards embarking for England.'

boomed to around 380,000 in May.

As 1919 drew to a close demobilisation was largely complete although there were still some serving abroad or involved in administering the returning soldiers who would not finally leave the colours until the following year. Industry was getting back on its feet despite the difficulties in some trades of converting back to a pre-war footing. The revolution that had been feared did not materialise. Most returning soldiers were more concerned with remembering those who did not return, the comradeship they had developed with those they had served with and the future for their families. For the working population there was now an expectation that the slums they lived in would be a thing of the past and their attention turned to the promises made by the government for better housing. Although the authorities had been prepared for the possibility of a socialist rising most returning soldiers gave radical politics a wide berth.

The Treaty of Versailles
The Armistice signed on 11 November 1918 only brought a suspension of hostilities not an end to the war. Germany was forced to withdraw its troops from France and Belgium within 15 days and Allied troops occupied the Rhineland (the western strip of Germany along the Rhine which bordered Belgium and Luxemburg). It was not until the following summer that the complex treaty had been finalised and was presented to the Germans who initially refused to sign, more because of the implication that the war was their fault rather than the huge costs they would have to pay. At 3.15pm on 28 June 1919 in the Hall of Mirrors in the Palace of Versailles, five years to the day after the assassination of the Austrian Archduke Ferdinand had set the wheels in motion towards war, Hermann Muller, the German Foreign Minister, and Johannes Bell, Minister of Colonial Affairs, signed the treaty for Germany. The war was now officially over.

War Memorials

Remembering the Dead

One legacy of the First World War which we can still see today in most towns, cities and villages is the memorials to the fallen. War memorials had been erected for centuries but these had generally recorded an important battle or conflict or a famous leader of men. By the time of the Boer War 1898-1902, attitudes towards men from lower ranks had changed and a number of local communities had raised memorials on which were carved the names of the men who did not return from South Africa.

The scale of loss after the First World War was vast compared to these earlier conflicts. For those families across Britain who had lost loved ones the ordeal was made more painful as the bodies of the deceased were not going to be brought home. From 1915 there was a ban on the return of the dead from the conflict zones because of the logistical problems involved, issues with health and the demoralising impact that thousands of bodies arriving on these shores would have had on the population at home. There are thousands of graves of soldiers and personnel who died during the First

World War in cemeteries in Britain but these are of men and women who passed away in military hospitals in this country, in training accidents, during air raids or were washed ashore after a naval incident. As

Coventry War Memorial was inaugurated in October 1927 by Field Marshall Douglas Haig. Money for this impressive Art Deco style monument was raised through a public appeal and within the base of its 90ft high structure is a Chamber of Silence in which the names of over 2,500 First World War victims are recorded.

31

Laurence Binyon's 1914 poem *For the Fallen* includes the following lines, which were widely used on gravestones and memorials of soldiers who died during the conflict:

They shall grow not old, as we that
*   are left grow old.*
Age shall not weary them, nor the
*   years condemn.*
At the going down of the sun and
*   in the morning,*
We will remember them.

The Commonwealth War Graves Commission has its origins in the tireless work of Fabian Ware. He dedicated himself to recording the graves of soldiers on the Western Front during the conflict and helped establish the Imperial War Graves Commission, now the Commonwealth War Graves Commission, in 1917. By 1918 they had identified nearly 600,000 graves and recorded over 550,000 casualties for whom no burial place was known. During the 1920s they laid out over 2,000 cemeteries in France, Belgium and in other conflict zones where the bodies could rest in peace alongside each other regardless of their rank. They also commissioned memorials for the hundreds of thousands of men who could not be identified (see *The Trench: Life and Death on the Western Front* for more information).

there were no regulations governing British casualties who died in this country they were usually buried at a site chosen by their family. There are also a number of graves for officers who died early in the war and whose bodies were repatriated by their families.

After the conflict it was decided that the war dead should remain on foreign fields despite many families expecting the bodies of loved ones to be repatriated. It was felt that because of the cost and difficulties that this would involve and in respect of the brotherhood which had developed between those who faced the horrors of the war together, their remains should be interred side by side in new cemeteries along the Western Front. There was hence a strong feeling in most communities in this country that there should be local memorials raised for the sake of those having to deal with the loss of a loved one without a grave to act as a focal point for their grief. They would also serve as a reminder of the contribution made by men and women during the conflict lest future generations should forget. Hence war memorials were raised during the 1920s in nearly every village, town and city across the country, usually from money raised by public subscription or from private individuals, to remember those who did not return.

It is estimated that around 70,000 memorials were raised, the great variety of their design recognising that these were personal to the community who chose and financed them. Many are in the form of a column, pillar or obelisk. Some have a gently stepped back upper section reflecting architectural fashion and columns often have a broken shaft which symbolises a life cut short. The Cenotaph in Whitehall, designed by the leading architect of the time, Sir Edwin Lutyens, was very influential

The Cenotaph in Whitehall, London was unveiled by King George V on 11 November 1920 in place of a near identical temporary structure designed by Sir Edwin Lutyens for the Victory Parade in July 1919. The cenotaph or empty tomb is the coffin shaped box at the top of the memorial, raised up upon the pylon or pillar of stone with the dates of the war carved above the wreaths which represent both victory and eternal life. It was never dedicated as not all of those it commemorates were Christian.

The Earl Haig Memorial in Whitehall was commissioned in 1928 shortly after his death and unveiled in time for Armistice Day 1937. The inscription on the base reads 'Field Marshal Earl Haig Commander-in-Chief of the British Armies in France 1915–1918'. Haig's own grave is marked by a simple War Graves Commission white gravestone at Dryburgh Abbey in the Scottish borders.

War memorials are more than just a record of lost members of the local community. Their style, size and symbolism reflects the way locals were dealing with their grief and how they viewed this most horrific of wars. During the centenary commemorations these memorials were being recorded and much of the information they hold is now available online. The following websites may be able to help with research (see also Further Information):
www.iwm.org.uk/memorials/search
www.roll-of-honour.com
www.pmsa.org.uk/pmsa-database/

in the design of monuments. Its simple form with an empty tomb raised upon a rectangular pillar and a stepped upper section had been planned and erected as a temporary structure in only two weeks before the Victory or Peace Day Parade in July 1919. It was decided afterwards that it should be replaced by an identical stone version as a national monument in time for the Armistice Day commemorations the following year.

The cross was another popular form of memorial, especially in smaller communities where they were erected on a plinth in churchyards or at a key location in a village. Many use traditional forms but some were based upon the Cross of Sacrifice designed by Sir Reginald Blomfield and used in many of the Commonwealth War Grave Commission's cemeteries. More ambitious designs included specially commissioned sculptures with figures specific to the subject of the memorial or chosen because they were deemed appropriate.

Many public bodies, companies and institutions erected plaques listing employees lost in the war. There are numerous offices, factories and railway stations which have memorials and plaques recording

The Belgian Gratitude Memorial, opposite Cleopatra's Needle, Victoria Embankment, London bears the inscription 'To the British nation from the grateful people of Belgium 1914-1918'. It was designed by Sir Reginald Blomfield with the bronze sculpture of a woman and children carrying garlands by Victor Rousseau. It was not only raised in gratitude for British efforts on the battlefield but also for the sheltering of thousands of Belgian refugees in this country during the war.

Pillars and obelisks with bronze sculpture were a popular and distinguished memorial for many towns and cities. These examples from Luton (left), Leeds (centre) and Lockerbie (right) are perhaps more notable for the seemingly endless lists of fallen soldiers which still remind us today of the devastating loss of life in the First World War.

Railway stations which were the headquarters of the numerous railway companies which operated at the time had memorials erected with roll calls of employees lost in the war. Waterloo Station was being redeveloped by the London and South Western Railway and the main entrance was built as a huge memorial arch (left) with the goddess of war on the left and the figure of peace on the right. Four plaques inside list over 500 employees who did not return. At Manchester Victoria Station (right) the Lancashire and Yorkshire Railway mounted seven plaques with the roll call of fallen staff below the tiled map of their network.

fallen colleagues. Some communities chose to dedicate a new building like a village hall or school as a war memorial with a metal plaque to record the fact. In other cases a recreational area or park was laid out with the dedication often recorded on a gateway or a memorial within the green space. Another common form was a new stained glass window in the local church, sometimes with the roll call of the fallen soldiers within the glass or on a separate plaque below.

War Graves Commission gravestones to three servicemen who died in this country during the First World War.

Coventry War Memorial Park was opened in 1922 but with council funds directed towards building homes it was not until later in the decade that the monument (page 31) was completed. Each tree planted was dedicated to an individual serviceman from the army, navy or air force with their names and rank recorded on these plaques at the base.

A granite obelisk unveiled in 1921 to the memory of the 66 employees of the Triumph and Gloria Companies, Coventry who died during the First World War.

Part of a cast iron memorial drinking fountain erected to the memory of the 45 staff of the Coventry Chain Company who were lost in the war. It was given to the city by the owner of the company in 1920.

The Victoria Cross is the highest military decoration for valour in the British and Commonwealth armies. In the four years of the First World War it was awarded 628 times, nearly half of the total number which have been awarded in its 150 year history. This plaque in the Coventry War Memorial Park records the heroics of Arthur Hutt VC (1889-1954) during the Battle of Passchendaele on 4 October 1917.

Stained glass windows in churches were another popular form of memorial. New designs were commissioned and the names of soldiers who did not return from the war listed on plaques below or within the glass as in this example at St John the Baptist church, Coventry.

The Bright New Future

1919-1921

In order to provide new housing for the returning heroes and keep the promise Lloyd George had made on the eve of the election in 1918, the government would have to solve a number of problems. New houses would be required in significant numbers in a short space of time in order to provide better accommodation for those who would move from the slums. However, around half the workers in the construction industry had left to fight in the war, meaning that there had been little or no house building for the last few years of the conflict so there was a backlog of existing projects. Along with the scarcity of labour there was also a shortage of materials, which had pushed up the cost of building houses, while the Rents and Mortgages Restriction Act had capped the amount landlords could charge. This made it unlikely that the private sector would be in a position to provide new housing at a low enough rent to help relieve the problem. The answer lay in passing legislation which would empower local authorities to build new houses and, by cutting out the profit formerly taken by private landlords and the charges for mortgages, would lower the rent and make them affordable to those trapped in poor housing.

The Tudor Walters Report

In 1917, when preparations were being made by the government for

The first 'homes for heroes', built after the war were termed 'cottages' and replicated many of the features found in pre war garden suburb projects. This included variety in form as with these houses in Bristol.

life after the war concluded, whether the country was victorious or not, Lloyd George's coalition established a committee to study the problem of providing housing with affordable rents and the form they should take. Under the chairman Sir John Tudor Walters, and guided by the experienced social housing architect Sir Raymond Unwin, the committee looked at ways by which spacious and light housing with proper sanitation and individual bedrooms could be built cost effectively. They were not only concerned with the appearance of the buildings, the layout of the interiors and the density of housing on the estates but also the practical methods by which construction costs could be lowered. The Tudor Walters Report, which was finally presented in November 1918, was so influential that it set the standard for much of the housing built up until the 1960s.

The plans recommended in the report reflected the design of pre-war garden suburbs. In the decade before the war this new form of estate with spacious plots, cottage style houses and wide streets with trees and green spaces had been built in a number of towns and cities. Although these were generally small in size, at Letchworth Garden City a full scale urban area had been planned. Raymond Unwin and his partner Barry Parker were invited to contribute to its design and to other schemes intended to improve working class housing financed by benevolent individuals and organisations like the Rowntrees at New Earswick near York and Henrietta Barnett at Hampstead

Housing in the 1920s was inspired by work at Letchworth Garden City (right) and in garden suburbs like Wavertree, Liverpool (above) built before the war.

Garden Suburb, London. The houses, usually termed cottages, had gardens front and back and were built in short rows or as semis. They had separate sculleries, inside flushing toilets, provision for a bath and at least two bedrooms upstairs.

Using these blueprints Unwin and the report's authors recommended that new urban estates should have around twelve houses per acre and eight in the country (40-80 per acre could be found in some old Victorian slum areas). This spacious layout allowed for front and rear gardens with room for tenants to grow vegetables and have fruit trees. Unlike most pre-war terraced housing which had rear extensions blocking air flow and light, these new structures were wider with larger areas of glass allowing sunlight to flood in. They would be set in pairs or rows of no more than six along wide avenues, crescents and cul de sacs. The rooms would be carefully planned within the main body of the house with three basic plans suggested. The most compact would have a floor area of around 850 sq ft, with a living room featuring a range on which the cooking could be done and a scullery behind for washing, laundry and bath night. The next size up had a separate bathroom, so the cooking would be done in the scullery with just a fireplace in the front living room. The largest had a separate parlour for study or family

meals and an upstairs bathroom with a total floor space of around 1,050 sq ft. Although the number of bedrooms could vary it was felt that the vast majority would have three. These plans were not just wishful thinking but incorporated practical tips on reducing construction costs and standardising components whilst bearing in mind that there would be both shortages of materials and labour to consider.

The Addison Act 1919

Christopher Addison was the talented son of a Lincolnshire farming family

Christopher Addison (1869-1951) was the Minister for Health who would put the recommendations of the Tudor Walters Report into action.

who after training at medical school in Sheffield and St Bartholomew's Hospital, London, became a doctor of notable repute. Yet this medical man was destined to take a new direction when after spending time working in some of the most desperately poor parts of London he moved into politics, seeing government as the place where he could be of greater influence. Addison's medical background was key in helping Lloyd George's 1911 National Insurance bill pass through Parliament and when the latter became Prime Minister his close associate was given the responsibility of planning for post war Britain. His government department was concerned with rebuilding and improving society at the end of hostilities and covered aspects including industrial relations, the role of women in society and improved housing.

In January 1919 Addison became President of the Local Government Board which would evolve into the new Ministry of Health later that year and would retain responsibility for social housing. The Board approved nearly all the recommendations in the Tudor Walters Report and with Addison at the helm finally put the ideas of the social improvers into legislation with the Housing and Town Planning Act finalised in July 1919. This instructed every local authority to 'consider the needs of their area with respect to the provision of houses for the working classes'. They had to report back within three months with their plans to build new estates, stipulating the

Once the euphoria of victory had died down those returning from the war talked little about their experiences to their families. The horrors they had witnessed would cloud the conscience of former soldiers and focus the minds of many on the value of the family and home. Those who carried the physical scars from the constant shelling on the Western Front not only had to adapt to life and work with a disability but also cope with the reaction their appearance might induce. Men with missing limbs, facial disfigurement or gaping wounds on the body were a common sight. Soldiers who suffered from the mental trauma of war could have a particularly hard time adapting to family life with little understanding of what they had endured and how to help with its effects. As a result children in the inter war period would often grow up innocent to what had happened and were particularly fascinated by the men they came across carrying the scars from the conflict. In Roald Dahl's memoirs, *Boy: Tales of Childhood*, the author describes his most feared teacher at school, Captain Hardcastle, a thin wiry man with a magnificent ginger moustache. He had a constant twitch and jerking action accompanied by snorting which humoured the pupils. Dahl described how rumour had it that it was caused by shellshock but the children were not sure what that was, 'We took it to mean that an explosive object had gone off very close to him with such an enormous bang that it had made him jump high in the air and he hadn't stopped jumping since.'

number of houses they intended to build, the amount of land required, the density of housing and the time it would take to complete.

The government would subsidise these schemes by covering the local authority for any loss incurred after rent and income from raising rates was taken into consideration, as long as they could prove they had kept a tight rein on construction expenses. It gave them the powers for compulsory purchase of land and then if necessary to be able to sell it to someone who would build the housing for them. There were also subsidies put in place for philanthropic societies to receive up to 30% of their initial budget to build new or convert old properties to help relieve housing problems

in addition to the work of the councils.

Part of the act covered local byelaws which were to be established to ensure that certain standards were maintained on the new estates. These included making sure only one family resided within a house and that the sexes were separated in the bedrooms. Regular inspections would have to be made to check there was adequate drainage, ventilation, room lighting and fire safety and that family members had access to the toilet, washing and cooking facilities and space for storing food.

With the passing of this act local authorities had not only the powers but also the financial clout to build working class housing on a large

Tightly packed straight rows of Victorian terraces with tall rear extensions (left) cast shadows and restricted light, which could make the streets and rear yards dark and unsanitary. The new spacious estates of the Addison Act had houses set width ways along curved roads with large gardens so all could share in the sunlight (right).

scale. They would take the lead in solving the housing problem for the returning soldiers. As the politician Lord Long stated, 'To let them come back from the horrible water-logged trenches to something little better than a pig-sty here would indeed be criminal on the part of ourselves, and would be a negation of all that had been said during the war.' With this in mind the government sought the ambitious target of building around 500,000 new homes under this important piece of legislation, better known today as the Addison Act.

Addison Act Houses

The houses built under the act largely followed the plans laid out in the Tudor Walters Report for spacious homes in bright and airy surroundings. One of the health issues which planners were keen to solve was the lack of light in the old terraces. They were too tightly packed together, had rear extensions which made the backs dark and were laid out with little consideration for exposure to the sun. The new plans allowed for spacious tree-lined streets with pavements and large green areas with the houses arranged so as to catch the sunlight. The street plans of the estates were full of curves and circles. Crescents were laid out with the gaps between filled by short cul-de-sacs and circuses (round open spaces) positioned at key junctions. These give inter-war

The Chapel Street Estate in Poplar, London, was the first built for the Borough Council under the Addison Act and was completed in 1921. It was designed by Sir Frank Baines, the architect for the Office of Works, which built the houses, as the council did not use their own workforce until the 1930s. The original concept of the garden suburb has been retained nearly 100 years later with these fine Neo Georgian style houses representing a high point in the drive to make 'Homes fit for Heroes'.

estates a distinctive appearance on a map.

The new semi-detached and terraced houses usually had hipped roofs, ones which slope on the front, back and sides. Sometimes these were tall structures covered in clay tiles, other times shallower pitched with slates. Both forms helped allow more light in between the houses. Rather than being long and thin in plan the new houses were wider with entrances either on the front or down the sides so doors faced each

44

other at the ends of a row or pair. Although many houses were intended to resemble old cottages with pebble-dashed walls and casement windows the style which would become dominant in early council housing was Neo Georgian. This revival of 18th century style was in fashion at the time and its plain walls with just a band of raised brickwork and the occasional decorative feature made it an economic form to use. Its boxy proportions and hipped roofs were closer to early 19th century suburban villas than tall Georgian terraces but the use of sash windows was appropriate.

Inside these more spacious and bright homes there would usually be two main rooms downstairs, with occasionally a third to be used as a parlour, a smart quiet room for reading and family occasions. The living room at the front in the smallest houses was designed to be used for preparing food and eating meals with a compact range built into the fireplace for cooking and boiling water. There would be a few chairs and some built in cupboards for storage. The scullery behind was for washing pans and clothes, with a copper (a metal vessel set in a brick casing with a fire below) to

Black Country Living Museum, Dudley, West Midlands: With the shortage of building materials which would last until the early 1920s and a limited number of skilled bricklayers (training ex-soldiers was a slow process) the Ministry of Health was keen to promote new ideas for non traditional building. There was plenty of capacity for the factory production of house parts using materials like concrete, cast iron and steel and the Ministry also put financial incentives in place. Although there had been some attempts to reduce the cost of building

before the war with cheaper forms of construction these non traditional houses built in the 1920s were experimental. Some used combinations of concrete, steel and timber with the house formed from vertical posts and infill panels, others were built using precast concrete posts and panels or had sections poured into shuttering on site. This cast iron house dating from 1919 from the Black Country Living Museum was built from iron panels bolted to a metal frame. By 1930 around 50,000 non traditional houses had been built but in most cases these were used by local authorities as a temporary measure while there was a shortage of bricklayers and they would soon return to traditional building methods.

heat water, a sink and draining board and some form of tin bath which could be placed on the floor for the weekly bath night. Most new houses were more spacious with the cooking and washing done in the rear room which would start to appear more like a kitchen, leaving the front living room with space for relaxing. These houses included a bathroom, a new feature to most tenants, with a permanently plumbed in bath. A separate flushing toilet was another much appreciated addition. Most houses had three bedrooms and unlike older working class properties which rarely had heating upstairs these would have a fireplace in one or two of the rooms. There would also be a larder or store built into the structure and somewhere close to the back door for keeping coal.

Building the first estates

The authorities first had to find plots of land which would be large enough to allow them to build these spacious new estates but also cheap enough so that the costs of purchasing it did not push the rents up beyond the means of those it was intended to relieve.

In Glasgow there had long been a crisis with housing the working classes. The 1861 census recorded that nearly 65% of the Scottish population were living in homes with only one or two rooms and in many cases containing families of five to ten people in these tiny spaces. There had been little improvement by the start of the First World War with around half the population still in this situation and nearly 70% in Glasgow, more than double that of London. The problems were highlighted in the Royal Commission on the Housing of the Industrial Population of Scotland which reported in 1917 recommending the provision of

In Manchester a report by the Housing Committee in 1920 estimated that around 17,000 new homes were required. They were granted 250 acres of land in rural Wythenshawe and after consulting Patrick Abercrombie, best known for his post Second World War planning of London, they made designs for a huge garden city. However there were numerous hold ups and objections from influential locals so that building of houses like those pictured here did not start until the 1930s.

In Leeds old back to backs, small terraces sharing the same rear wall with no rear gardens or yard, made up a large proportion of the housing stock. Some of the better built versions are still standing today as pictured here.

municipal housing at affordable rents and helping to shape the legislation which followed. The task of the authorities in implementing the Addison Act in Glasgow was made harder because land was more expensive than in most other cities and local building regulations demanded a higher, and hence more expensive, standard of construction than elsewhere. Rents as a result had been higher even before the war with tenants paying on average over four shillings a week for a small home compared with just over three shillings in the industrial cities of Northern England.

Most councils found similar restrictions in the old centres and began looking beyond the traditional urban boundary at the farmland and old country estates which bordered it. With land values still low in many rural areas after years of agricultural depression these swathes of cheap fields and parkland around the

towns and cities also helped make the planned spacious housing cost effective. In Wolverhampton space was limited in the town so the estate at Birches Barn was built on nearby farmland, at Oxley a golf course was purchased and the Parkfield Road site was a former colliery. The first Addison Act houses were ready to be moved into as early as November 1919 and over 500 had been completed after five years.

In Leeds there was also an urgent need for new estates. Here too the existing city area was tightly packed with a very large proportion of back to back housing of variable quality. The council therefore had to look further afield and bought up farmland at sites at Meanwood, Middleton, Wyther Park, Cross Gates and Hawksworth. Again, with the shortage of skilled bricklayers the council took the decision to system build some of the houses from prefabricated concrete

In Bristol the council experimented with concrete and steel houses on the first estates. They promised to be cheaper to construct and did not require skilled bricklayers who were still in short supply. Through the 1920s they erected over 1,000 using a system of reinforced concrete posts and panels, which could be offered at a lower rent to tenants. Problems with insulation, condensation and the spalling (water damage) of the concrete has resulted in some being demolished and those which survive like these examples on the Sea Mills Estate have been partially rebuilt.

parts and by 1924 nearly 3,500 new homes had been completed, half of which had been constructed in this way.

The council in Bristol had lagged behind other cities in the provision of housing before the war, providing no family houses and a limited number of tenements for single men. However in 1918 they purchased around 700 acres of farmland around the edge of the city in anticipation of new housing schemes. The first of these were built in 1919 at Hillfields Park to the east and at Sea Mills to the west, the latter having its first sod of earth cut by Christopher Addison in June of that year. Along with Knowle to the south of the city which was to develop into the largest estate, these first houses were built along garden city lines with spacious accommodation and even

features like bay windows which were a rarity in these cost effective homes. Despite the ambitions of this first post war scheme in Bristol only around 1,200 of the planned 5,000 houses were built.

As with other cities the London County Council looked to greenfield sites outside the area of the authority in addition to developing pockets of land within. The scale of their plans was such that additional funding would be required; London Housing Bonds were launched in 1919 by which the public were encouraged to invest in a scheme 'as safe as houses' and which resulted in raising around £4 million. New estates were planned around the capital but the largest and most ambitious was to be at Becontree in Dagenham. Farms were compulsorily purchased by the LCC and building work began

The Sea Mills estate in Bristol was one of the first major housing schemes for the city instigated by the 1919 Addison Act. The estate was inspired by pre-war garden suburbs and included a number of private houses as well as council provided ones, with some of the best examples along St Edyth's Road, pictured here. The cost of building these houses though was high and the rents charged on streets like this were still beyond the purse of many working families.

This plaque in Beechen Drive, Bristol commemorates the building of the first houses in the city in 1919 under the National Housing Scheme, as the Addison Act was referred to at the time.

in 1921. After only ten years or so over 25,000 houses had been built, providing accommodation for around 100,000 people.

Other sites chosen were in existing built up areas. In Poplar, which included the Isle of Dogs, there was already a problem with overcrowding and nearly a quarter of the population lived in accommodation with at least two people per room. The local

49

borough council started on the first estate at Chapel Street in October 1919 with good quality three and four bedroomed houses set along paved, tree-lined streets. They were also keen to lay on electricity for lighting in all their houses although gas was still the usual choice at this date. This little estate of Neo Georgian houses and low rise flats were built at a density of 15 dwellings per acre, not quite the recommended twelve but more spacious than the estates which would follow it.

The end of the Addison Act

The passing of the Addison Act and the first houses which were erected under its powers were an important step forward in raising the standard of living. Private industry had failed in most cases over the previous century to provide affordable housing and local authorities, brought up on an ethos of 'self help', had done little until living conditions had become so critical that they had been forced to step in. Now in the euphoria of

The plan of a larger Addison Act council house based upon an example from Poplar, London. The extra space allowed planners to fit in a parlour at the front of the house, a room which most working class families treasured and reserved for Sunday meals and special occasions. A small plumbed in bath and wash basin were separated from the flushing toilet with the front door set to one end of the house, a common feature of inter-war council housing. Everyday meals would have been taken in the living room with washing and cooking mostly performed in the kitchen/ scullery behind. Four bedrooms upstairs was a luxury for most families who were used to sharing one large sleeping space, the fact two of them had heating was a real bonus although fires were usually only lit when someone elderly or infirm was using them.

The Becontree estate, Dagenham, London was the largest public housing estate in the world. Between 1921 and 1937 over 26,000 homes were erected housing around 115,000 people. The Addison Act allowed the London County Council to build outside of its boundary so they planned this massive suburban cottage estate on an area of four square miles in the then rural districts of Dagenham, Barking and Ilford. Financing came in part from the London Housing Bonds and the building costs were reduced by buying materials and fittings in bulk, with some imported from the continent. A dock was set aside and a special railway built into the estate to bring these to site. The new houses had gas and electricity, inside flushing toilets, a fitted bath and front and back gardens giving them space to grow their own vegetables and fruit trees. Public facilities were built as the estate developed but pubs themselves were initially banned.

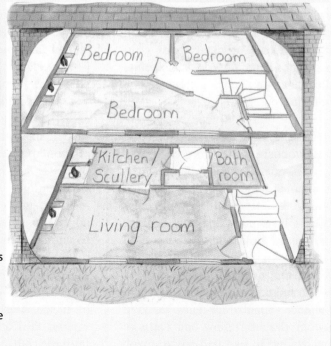

A plan of a smaller council house from Poplar in which the range was built into the living room where the family cooked and ate their meals. The scullery behind was used for washing clothes, cleaning dishes and housing a tin bath which would be put on the floor and filled with hot water from the copper in the corner.

The Housing Manual was the result of the Tudor Walters Report and was issued in 1919. It formed the basis of the plans made by local authorities for the 'homes fit for heroes' with drawings of suggested designs and layouts of houses and recommended minimum dimensions. However by 1921, as pressure mounted on the costs of the housing scheme, the Ministry of Housing instructed local authorities that the dimensions listed in the manual should be used as a maximum rather than minimum. This was the first step in the cutting back of the ambitions of a bright future laid out in the wake of the First World War.

The Addison Oak on the square at the centre of the Sea Mills estate, Bristol was planted by Christopher Addison when he came to cut the first sod of earth on the site in 1919.

victory and fired up by the desire to reward returning soldiers, or at least stave off any revolutionary ideas, they had proved that attractive and sanitary 'cottages' could be provided if there was sufficient funding in place. Unfortunately it was at this point that the Addison Act became unstuck.

Despite being Liberal Party leader, Lloyd George's coalition government was dominated by the Conservatives. They still generally believed that housing should only be financed by the public purse to provide sanitary accommodation of the minimum standard for those affected by slum clearance and Addison's plans began to seem extravagant. Once the fear of revolution had subsided and the hard economic facts of how much this scheme was going to cost

became apparent they started raising objections and in April 1921 Addison was moved from the Ministry of Health. When the Cabinet voted to end his housing scheme a few months later he resigned from the government.

When all the projects which had been financed by this groundbreaking act were completed the total number of around 200,000 houses fell well short of the half a million which were required. Although many had regarded the public authorities' involvement in housing as a temporary measure until the private sector was back on its feet, there was still a desperate shortage of affordable accommodation. With a growing number of young couples marrying once men had returned from the war and with the slum areas in most cities still to be effectively tackled, the pressure was on and in some areas had even grown despite the houses built. There was also a new and major issue which would shape any further actions: the economy.

The bathroom was the one room all tenants seem to have agreed was a major improvement in their life. Most were utilitarian and tightly packed, some with the w.c. in the same room as in this example at the Black Country Living Museum. Others still had a portable bath in the scullery filled by a syphon pipe from the copper.

Larger houses had a separate scullery or kitchen in which the preparation and cooking of meals could take place alongside the washing. The copper, a bricked in metal vessel heated below by a small fire (seen here in the corner) provided the large quantities of hot water required on wash day.

Economic Crisis
1922–1930

Once British industry had resolved the initial problems of supply and had returned to peacetime production it was met with a boom in demand. There was an assumption amongst many that the country would shortly return to its traditional position of industrial supremacy.

However, many factors had now changed and the signs were there long before the war. Competing nations had more modern and efficient production techniques and were quick to seize opportunities in both traditional heavy and the new light industries. During the war Britain's existing customers had sourced their supplies from elsewhere as production was switched to the war effort, and when the conflict ended many of them did not return. By 1920 demand began to drop especially in textiles, iron, steel, coal and shipbuilding. Economic growth stagnated and by 1921 there was deflation. As a result unemployment rose sharply to over 10% and remained fairly high through the rest of the decade. At the same time income tax had risen by over 30% since 1919. This was particularly cruel on many of the returning soldiers who were promised a 'Land Fit for Heroes' only to find themselves still stuck in poor housing and now without a job. In the aftermath of the war there was little assistance beyond basic financial aid for those who had suffered as a result of

Towns and cities involved in the production of chemicals, electrical appliances, aeroplanes, and motor cars were more likely to expand and have large scale private as well as local authority housing estates during the inter war years. Much of this new building was concentrated in the Midlands and South East, especially around London where the leafy suburbs filled with semi detached houses, as pictured here, expanded at a rapid rate. Those areas reliant upon the old heavy industries, especially coal, tended to suffer the most as there was little investment and few alternative industries resulting in high long term unemployment and lower wages.

the conflict or for the families of men who did not return. Even those who were fit and well often found themselves struggling with life in the slums, the effects of the flu epidemic and by the early 1920s, rising unemployment.

Looking to the private sector

In January 1921 the newspaper proprietor Lord Rothermere launched the Anti-Waste League, a political party which publicly campaigned against what they saw as inappropriate levels of government spending at a time of economic strife. They particularly focused upon the high levels of income tax and the huge expenditure bill on the social housing scheme. As pressure grew, Lloyd George appointed Eric Geddes in August 1921 as chairman of a committee to see where cuts could be made. The report of the Committee on National Expenditure was published in the following year and the housing budget was severely cut back by what became known as the 'Geddes Axe'. The schemes planned under the Addison Act were slowly wound up. In October 1922 Lloyd George was ousted as Prime Minister and in the subsequent general election the Conservatives under Andrew Bonar Law won an overall majority, bringing an end to the wartime coalition government.

The new government looked to the private sector to help reduce the

Emigration: In some parts of the country where unemployment was rapidly escalating, migration or emigration were serious options which could help relieve the pressure for new housing. During the 1920s there was a notable shift, principally of young skilled workers from old shipbuilding, coal mining and similar trades in the North, into the new light industries of the South East and Midlands. In Scotland during the 1920s over half a million left for England or overseas destinations especially Canada, Australia, and South Africa. This represented nearly 20% of the working population north of the border and around 8% of the total population in just ten years. Economic depression was the driving force as the number in shipbuilding for instance dropped from around 100,000 in 1920 to just 10,000 ten years later. The advantage of reducing the urban population in some areas was not lost on the authorities and the government also saw it as a way to bolster up the British Empire. In 1921 they established the Overseas Settlement Committee which gave ex-servicemen and women free passage to the Dominions with over 80,000 taking up the offer before it closed two years later. The Empire Settlement Act of 1922 also provided funds to assist others to emigrate around the British Empire and by the mid 1930s over 400,000 had used this scheme's subsidies to start a new life overseas. These not only included skilled workers but also female domestic staff who were in great demand around the Empire.

housing shortage. Since 1915 rent restrictions had been in place which controlled the amount tenants could be charged, hence there had been little incentive for private builders to erect working class housing. The removal of these restrictions would be a highly controversial move and instead the new Minister of Health, Neville Chamberlain, introduced the 1923 Housing Act in which subsidies were made available for the private sector to encourage them to tackle the problem. It was envisaged that this would boost the supply such that within a couple of years rent restrictions could be lifted (they actually remained in place until 1933 and then in revised forms until the 1980s). There were subsidies available for continued local authority housing but they were much reduced and so councils were forced to cut back their planning ambitions and reduce the size of the houses built. In order to receive government funding, the maximum floor area of a two storey house was now 950 sq ft which had been a minimum size for many of the houses under the Addison Act. From now on the private sector would become more involved in providing housing for the working classes although not on the scale Chamberlain envisaged. Nor were the houses they built always to the same standard as those in the public sector as speculative builders would trim the dimensions

Neville Chamberlain (1869-1940)
Although the son of a politician, Neville Chamberlain spent most of his early career in business, even spending six years unsuccessfully trying to establish a plantation in the Bahamas. His ventures were more fruitful back home and in 1911 he was elected to Birmingham City Council and became Chairman of the Town Planning Committee. In this role he put plans in place to try to tackle the poor housing in much of the city where around 50,000 houses still did not have running water, only for the outbreak of war to cut short his plans. After winning a parliamentary seat in 1918 he became chairman of the Unhealthy Areas Committee and sought to continue this work when he became Minister of Health in 1923; the housing act he introduced that year is still referred to by his name.

and simplify the layout to reduce construction costs and maintain profits.

The Wheatley Housing Act 1924

In May 1923 Prime Minister Bonar Law was diagnosed with cancer and immediately stepped down. His replacement as leader, Stanley Baldwin, sought a mandate for his position and went to the polls in December but his rash decision backfired and he lost the party's majority. In January the following year Labour under Ramsey MacDonald formed a new government. The new Minister of Health was John Wheatley and he immediately set about creating legislation to tackle the ongoing housing crisis. He sought a solution on a larger scale and longer term, looking not just at the financial support and cost of supplies but also improving training so that there would be a workforce able to step up the rate of construction. The standard of the houses would maintain the quality set by the Addison Act but were of the reduced size established by Chamberlain, although Wheatley maintained that they would be 'homes not hutches'. When the act was passed it put the emphasis back upon the public sector with subsidies in place to encourage local councils to build large scale working class estates again. The aim was to triple the rate of construction so that just under half a million houses would be built each year by the mid 1930s.

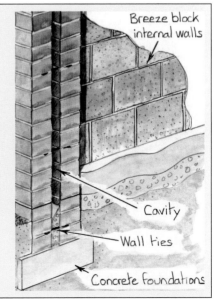

House Construction

Despite experiments with alternative materials and methods of construction most houses built in the 1920s and 1930s still had brick walls. The major difference compared with houses built before the war was the widespread use of cavity walls, an inner and outer skin held together by metal ties with a void between which helped insulate the building and reduce rain penetration. This method had been used in some coastal regions since the late 19th century but now was becoming the standard method of constructing walls. These sat on firm concrete foundations adding stability to the structure. Breeze blocks, made from cement mixed with waste from burning coal or coke, were a cheap and quick way to form walls although doubts over their durability meant they were usually used for internal walls only.

Breeze block internal walls

Cavity

Wall ties

Concrete foundations

57

John Wheatley, unlike his predecessors at the Ministry of Health, had no privileged background. His desire to improve the plight of those stuck in slum conditions came from personal experience. Wheatley was the son of an Irish miner who moved his family to Lanarkshire when he was only seven. Here they were only able to afford a single room shared with his brothers, sisters and lodgers with a communal toilet, no running water, and beds which were rolled up each morning. Wheatley worked down the pits from the age of 12 but through self education was able to establish his own printing company and eventually became a successful businessman. This helped finance his political activities in Glasgow where the chronic housing conditions were one of his major concerns and he played a part in the 1915 rent strikes which forced the introduction of national rent controls. This passionate socialist believed the answer to the housing problem lay with government and that if the profit made by private landlords was eliminated and loans were available interest free then good quality municipal housing could be provided. The act Wheatley introduced in 1924 was built upon these ideas and upon his experience in Glasgow and would help finance the building of around half a million council houses.

War Pensions. The dependants of servicemen who were killed during the war received a war pension. How much money each family would receive was evaluated individually and depended upon the number of children. The pension was paid to the wife but was reduced when each child reached the age of 16. Those men who had been unable to continue with military service or other work due to injuries incurred in the war were also entitled to a pension, usually a percentage of the normal award and assessed annually by inspectors. This included those who had suffered mental issues as a result of the war although there was no guarantee that they would receive a pension and many claims were rejected. However, those who had married a soldier who had a disability that was known to them before they wed would not get the pension when that soldier died. This caused much anger amongst families as they had been encouraged to tie the knot by the authorities after the war but upon their husband's sudden death were suddenly unable to support themselves and many faced eviction and hardship. War pension cards and ledgers which recorded personal details about the soldiers and their dependants are now held by the Western Front Association. More information on accessing these can be found at www.westernfrontassociation.com.

In Poplar, London, new cottage estates were now built with the houses more tightly packed together and smaller in size, with many only having two rather than three bedrooms. Blocks of flats were also built by the LCC to house families evicted from slum areas. Birchfield House, pictured here, was one such example completed in 1927 with 40 individual flats (identified in alternative colours on the plan) intended to house up to 200 people. Each one had gas for a stove in the main living room and a fire in a bedroom. Electricity was laid on but initially was only used for the lighting in the communal passageways. Each family had its own toilet and scullery but these were positioned on the other side of the passageways (in white on the plan). Next to them were the washrooms which had a metal bath and a copper for washing clothes but were shared between two and three families. This simplified design meant in theory that lower rents could be charged, however they worked out to be very similar to flats built by the local borough council which had better facilities. The original layout of these flats, as shown here in a section of the plans, has since been reconfigured.

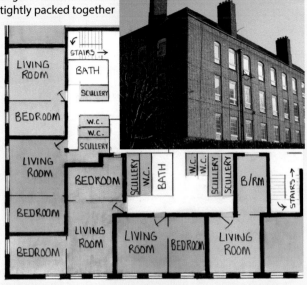

Across the country existing projects received a boost and new ones were put in motion. The Conservative council in Liverpool had been at the forefront of municipal housing before the war and had built the most houses under the Addison Act. Now, in the wake of the Wheatley Act they purchased over 600 acres on the edge of the city and began building the Norris Green Estate at such a rapid rate that it had a population of around 25,000 by 1930.

In Wolverhampton the council began the construction of the Low Hill and Bushbury Estates with over 2,000 houses erected by 1927. Bristol's authorities continued with their existing sites using the new legislation to construct just short of 10,000 homes by the mid 1930s. In London work on the huge Becontree Estate continued apace while other projects like the attractive Arts and Crafts inspired Dover House Estate in Putney were completed.

59

The Low Hill and Bushbury Estates, Wolverhampton were much larger in scale than the earlier projects built under the Addison Act. Between 1925 and 1929 the local authority built thousands of new three bedroom houses over fields to the north west of the town, most of them still having a parlour in addition to the scullery and living room. The estate also included shops around the green space in the centre of the estate (top) and more unusually a public house (bottom) which has since been converted into apartments.

Sash windows (with two glazed frames called sashes, the lower one of which slides vertically up behind the upper) were often fitted into new council houses during the 1920s (top). Despite being old fashioned and having more complicated workings they could be cheaper to supply than the simple hinged casement windows (bottom) which were fitted to most private housing at the time.

Metal framed windows had been widely used in commercial properties during the Victorian period and were installed in many of the munitions factories during the First World War. After the war the leading manufacturer of steel frames, Crittall Windows, expanded their offering in the domestic market and produced large quantities of 'cottage windows' for

CRITTALL WINDOWS

Will always work properly.
Last far longer than wood.
Are thoroughly weather-tight.
Do not swell, warp or shrink.
Can be cleaned from inside.
Have forged bronze fittings.

THE **CRITTALL**

MANUFACTURING CO LTD

HEAD OFFICE ✦ 210 HIGH HOLBORN ✦ WC1

council houses built under the various housing acts during the inter war years. They also provided windows for the booming private sector with modern designs featuring thin steel horizontal bars and geometric patterns. Their streamlined bay windows with curved ends are particularly distinctive of the 1930s Art Deco style homes. The company also built a large workers' housing estate at Silver End, south east of Braintree, Essex with modern style homes featuring flat roofs and Crittall's metal framed windows.

Rural poverty

If progress in solving the housing shortage was considered slow by many town dwellers in the 1920s then the situation in the countryside was even worse. With the focus on the urban masses agricultural labourers could find themselves left behind in the queue to get a better home. Their situations could vary dramatically. Some lived in well built housing provided by the estate which gave them permanent employment. Others were still stuck in tumbledown cottages with chronic damp and no electricity or gas, struggling to make ends meet with seasonal jobs. In some areas like Norfolk appalling conditions could be found and the promise of new village housing for these poor families was being held up by red tape, a lack of materials and rising costs which meant new cottages would be beyond the rent which they could afford.

In 1916 Mrs Willie James, the daughter of a Scottish aristocrat and organiser of infamous extravagant parties, established the Housing Association for Officers' Families. It would provide accommodation at low rents for the families of deceased or disabled officers or those in financial difficulties. It was not until 1929 that a similar organisation was set up specifically for ordinary soldiers. Douglas Haig Memorial Homes was established in memory of the former head of the army who had died in the previous year, with similar charitable intentions. Now known as Haig Housing and also incorporating the HAOF it has built up a stock of nearly 1,500 properties across the country offering affordable homes to ex-servicemen and their families, including special accommodation for those wounded in war.

The British Legion

In many cases it was down to local groups and individuals to try and help alleviate the problems of ex-servicemen and their families who found themselves destitute or down on their luck. One such individual was Lance Bombardier Tom Lister who had been invalided out of the war in 1916. He established the British National Federation of Discharged and Demobilized Sailors and Soldiers and found accommodation for ex-servicemen and their families by promising willing landlords that he would maintain their properties for them. He also set up soup kitchens and even convinced Burtons, the well known tailors, to give him suits for soldiers to use at interviews. Douglas Haig, the victorious leader of the British Army, had also retained a keen interest in the welfare of the soldiers who had served under him. He helped bring together the four main charitable groups which were supporting ex-servicemen and along with Tom Lister formed the British Legion. On 15 May 1921 at the Cenotaph in Whitehall the agreement between the parties was sealed with Tom Lister becoming its first chairman. Haig, who was its first president, also established the Haig Fund to raise financial support for ex-servicemen, chiefly by the selling of poppies which had the fund's name in the centre until they merged with the British Legion.

London County Council and the local borough authorities however faced difficulties in housing families on the limited pockets of land available within the metropolis and so began to build blocks of flats as a solution. As the slums were cleared it was these brick-built five storey tenements which became a common sight around the capital.

The problems with the new estates

Those homes fit for heroes which were erected in the 1920s may have been inspired by a need to reward returning soldiers and stave off the threat of revolution but it was quickly becoming apparent that only certain types of family were benefiting from them. Despite the attempts to build houses more cheaply the low density planning, sturdy structures and spacious interiors made the completed homes relatively expensive to rent. In Leeds for instance, where there

Most estates had strict rules on the cleaning of houses, maintaining boundaries and the appearance of the gardens. Inspectors would make regular visits to ensure the property was cleaned properly, maintenance was being kept up and that the family were adhering to the regulations. Tenants were not allowed to change the layout of the house and there were restrictions on how the garden should be used. Even the height of the hedges was set on many estates. On the Becontree Estate there was a rule stating that 'the tenant shall be responsible for the orderly conduct of his children on any part of the Estate' and the council would charge them for any damage the little ones caused. Failure to keep up these standards could in extreme cases lead to eviction, with only a week's notice given in many cases.

were still large swathes of compact back to backs which could be rented for as little as 5 shillings a week, the charge of over 15 shillings for an out of town council house was beyond many families. There were even big differences between the various council estates; in Poplar new houses could be rented for between 13 and 18 shillings a week while those built by the LCC out in the suburbs would cost another 5 shillings on top of that.

The more compact houses built under the Wheatley Act were generally

In this estate built in the 1920s in the south of Manchester the road was named after Christopher Addison.

cheaper to rent than the earlier ones and those made from concrete or steel cheaper still. Despite this in most cases the new houses were only let to those who had a permanent skilled job, like teachers, shopkeepers, civil servants and transport workers. Not only were these families most likely to pass the council's stringent tests before a house would be allocated but they were the ones who could afford the higher rent. The country of birth of applicants could also influence the decision on who would be offered a new house or flat. In London the LCC gave preference to British families from 1923, while some borough councils even refused to offer ethnic minorities a new home altogether.

Most families who moved out of cramped and unsanitary terraces into the new suburban cottages liked the space and features they found in their new homes. The bathrooms and flushing toilets which most houses had were especially appreciated. However there were problems. With their jobs back in the city centre many workers now had a long commute and had to find the money for trains or trams, adding more pressure to their weekly budget.

The houses also came with strict rules on maintenance so took more time and money to heat, clean and keep the gardens trim. In the rush to build

In Bristol the largest council estate at Knowle on the south east edge of the city had begun under the Addison Act. The spacious cottage style houses set along a wide tree lined street in this photo were from this first phase of building. The next houses built under the Wheatley Act were less generous in their size and are more densely fitted together but still retain some variety in their form and areas of greenery.

houses many of the planned facilities like shops, churches and community halls were not in place when families moved in. The local pub which had often been the centre of social life in the city was banned from many of these new suburban council estates.

They also found that there was a less than warm welcome from some of the private housing nearby. In Downham, Kent a high wall topped with broken glass was built across the road linking the new council estate to Bromley to prevent its residents passing through the neighbouring private estate! Hence families could find their new homes lonely and often felt cut off from the tight knit community back in the slums where everything they needed was just around the corner. It was not unusual for some to pack up their belongings and move back to their old terraced homes which were significantly cheaper and where they would be surrounded by familiar faces.

Despite the problems with the new estates and the state of the economy the rate of building new homes did increase. Under the Wheatley Act around half a million new homes were built and the concept and financial support of council-provided housing became more embedded. The Labour-led coalition only lasted until the end of 1924 but Chamberlain, who was restored to the position of Minister of Health in the new Conservative government, maintained the rate of progress. When Labour won the election in 1929 John Wheatley, having fallen out with the leadership over the General Strike three years earlier, was not offered a position and died the following year. He did not live to see the subsidies he introduced be abolished in 1933 as in the wake of a faltering economy and rising unemployment it was viewed as too expensive.

In the small mill town of Leek, Staffordshire the first houses which were provided by the council were a row of wooden huts which had been bought off the government and converted into dwellings. Brick-built houses were soon being erected on small pockets of land around the edge of the town, one group on a former glebe of the nearby church and named Glebeville. The largest estate to the east of the town was Abbotsville where around 300 houses were built during the 1920s. To make the houses more affordable cheap bricks were used to face all sides with a breeze block inner wall and even the ends of the rafters were left exposed along the eaves. Inside most had a large living room, a scullery to the rear with a downstairs flushing toilet, and three bedrooms upstairs with a permanent bath and wash basin. This example is very rare in retaining its original windows and doors.

The Women's Institute originated in the First World War, as a way of encouraging countrywomen to meet together to share their knowledge of growing and preserving food at a time of great hardship. The very first meeting was held in Wales in 1915, at Llanfair PG on Anglesey, and more institutes were quickly formed, the first in England being at Singleton in Sussex. By the end of 1917, there were enough up and running to be able to form a National Federation of Women's Institutes, under the chairmanship of Lady Denman. After the war the Federation took over all responsibility for the organisation from the Board of Agriculture, with the help of a continuing government grant of funds. With the extension of the vote to women aged over 30 and possessing property in 1918, and to all women over 21 in 1928, political parties found it necessary to listen to what women were concerned about. It was not long before the women of the WIs found a new political voice that helped them move beyond an interest in home and family, and at the AGM in 1918 a resolution echoed the concerns of families across the land in urging local authorities to take advantage of the scheme for state-aided housing. By 1920 there was a clear desire for women to become involved in solving the complex social issues that followed the war and members were being encouraged to stand for Parish and District Councils and particularly for the local committees dealing with health and housing. In 1921 WI member Margaret Winteringham became only the second woman to be elected to Parliament as MP for Louth. In the two decades between the wars, WI members became involved in issues as diverse as housing, domestic water supplies in rural areas, sexual health, and unemployment, and by 1933 there were over 5,000 institutes in operation.

Lady Denman (1884-1954) was born Gertrude (Trudie) Mary Pearson, daughter of Baron Cowdray, oil magnate and newspaper baron. She married the 3rd Baron Denman in 1903 and by 1911 was supporting him as Governor General of Australia, returning to England in 1914. A woman of great business sense and sympathy with the concerns and hardships of the rural community, she spent her life promoting the capacity of women to handle their own affairs and to take their place in political life. She was the guiding light of the Women's Institute movement from the beginning and in 1939 became Director of the Women's Land Army; she was awarded the Grand Cross of the British Empire in 1951. In the 1940s Marcham Park, near Abingdon, was purchased partly by WI funding and named Denman College, in her honour. It remains today at the heart of WI education and affection.

The Party's Over
The Stately Home's struggle for survival

While the focus of the authorities was firmly on building houses to solve overcrowding in the poorer urban districts, there were also great changes afoot at the other end of the social spectrum. Many of those who were born into wealth were suddenly to find their luxury carpets pulled from beneath their feet as their stately homes turned into unbearable tax burdens. The situation was made worse for some as the young heirs on whom the future of their estates rested had been killed on the Western Front by bombs and bullets which had no respect for social standing. Just as the urban landscape was to change so rapidly in these inter war years, so rural communities faced massive upheaval and new opportunities as the country house which their lives had formerly revolved around was sold or even destroyed.

The landed classes had for centuries held power based upon their position in Parliament. This was guaranteed by being able to control the voters who lived on their estates, so the land they owned was usually a solid investment. This system began to break down during the 19th century as the reforming of the electoral system and new taxation aimed at those with wealth were introduced. In addition, cheap food imports from America and around the Empire from the 1870s caused a depression in domestic agriculture resulting in a drop in revenue from estate farms and the value of land. Rich industrialists and men of finance were ready to step in and snap up failing estates while other families married their children into this new money or began investing in stocks to bolster their accounts. Country house life in the years immediately prior to the war gave the outward appearance of continued opulence and splendid parties, yet underneath their future existence was already being undermined.

The sons of wealthy landowners, industrialists and bankers being educated at leading public schools were amongst the most enthusiastic for the war and thousands signed up excitedly, innocent to the horrors which awaited them. Unfortunately, as officers on the Western Front they were usually the first out of the trenches when the whistles sounded to attack and were ruthlessly mown down by the first hail of bullets and

Devonshire House was built in the 1730s as a palatial urban residence for the Dukes of Devonshire. It was both home for the family when parliament was sitting and a glorious venue for entertaining with balls, concerts and parties held within its grand suites of rooms. For nearly two centuries it was a major centre of London society. After the First World War though the 9th Duke of Devonshire was faced with death duties and a long standing family debt to pay. These huge sums required the family to sell off property and with the declining influence of the aristocracy in political circles a valuable London house like this was an easy way to raise the funds required. It was sold to developers who were only interested in the 3 acres of prime land and promptly demolished the Palladian mansion. All that survives today are the gates which were relocated to Green Park and the wine cellar which now houses part of Green Park Station. Nearly all of the other grand aristocratic town houses in London have since gone or have been converted to commercial or public use.

shells. During the war Cambridge University suffered around 8,500 casualties, about two thirds of all those who signed up, with over half of these never returning. Oxford lost over 2,000 men and boys, around a fifth of all the members who signed up. Lord Cawley, MP for Prestwich lost three of his four sons in the war; his youngest Oswald died in August 1918 only six months after being elected to his father's seat in Parliament, where he never had the opportunity to serve. Their father paid for a new ward at Ancotes Hospital, Manchester in memory of his three boys.

The loss of so many young heirs was more than just an emotional blow to their families. Their prospective marriages to wealthy brides would have been vital to bring revenue into many estates and they would have been expected to take over its management when their fathers died. Haldon House in Devon was the home of James FitzGerald Bannatyne, a rich flour merchant who helped finance Marconi's early work with radio, some experiments taking place in the hills around his mansion. Bannatyne died in 1915 so the estate passed to his son but he was killed in action in France in the following year. His widow put the house up for sale as soon as the war ended.

Those from aristocratic ranks who

did survive the war returned to a home life which was to change more radically than that of some of the privates they had been in charge of. A large number of country houses had been turned into military camps, hospitals and convalescence homes during the conflict and after four years of heavy use and neglected maintenance many of these would require expensive repairs when they were handed back. Wealthy families suddenly found a chronic shortage of the staff they needed to run the house and estate. As the government looked to raise money to help pay off the colossal costs from the war they raised taxation, which would hit the well-off the hardest. At the beginning of the 20th century the owners of country house estates were being taxed at just under 10%, but after the war this annual bill nearly tripled. The biggest problem for most estates was death duties, charged when the head of the family passed away, and they were often the final hammer blow which forced the family to take drastic action. Some kept their most favoured house and sold off other properties, especially those in London.

Many families reduced the size of their main house so that fewer staff would be required to run it. Service wings were demolished, new kitchens built and labour saving appliances installed. Money could also be raised by selling off fittings like wood panelling, fireplace surrounds or decorative features and treasured

Country houses had been run as a self supporting unit. Behind all the glorious rooms for entertaining guests and accommodating the family were service areas and outbuildings where meals could be prepared and cooked, beer brewed, dairy products made, and even ice for chilling the food stored. This efficient system relied upon a skilled team of staff which could number in the hundreds working very long hours with little opportunity to venture away from their servants quarters. Even when the country house had its most glorious Indian summer in the decades before the First World War there had been a growing problem in finding good staff. Now the war was over country house owners found not only had they lost many good men who had fought in the war but also the army of women who made up the backbone of their staff were reluctant to come back. In the munitions factories during the war they had been better paid, had enjoyed canteens and recreation facilities and had time and money to go out after work and socialise. The Ministry of Reconstruction were keen to get domestic staff off the donation and back into work so applied pressure while at the same time encouraged those who employed them to improve working conditions. By May 1919 around 65,000 women had gone back into domestic service but there were many others who still refused and gave up the donation. This ever worsening problem in finding staff to live and work in these often remote grand houses was another reason which convinced many of their owners to sell them off.

Sutton Scarsdale had been bought by the son of Sir Richard Arkwright, the inventor of the water frame, in 1824 and remained in the family up to the end of the First World War. Its last owner William Arkwright had been partially paralysed when young and had had no children to inherit the house so decided in the wake of rising taxation to sell up. His main interest in the estate were the mineral rights in this expanding coal mining district. The industrialisation of the area would however lessen the appeal of Sutton Scarsdale to potential buyers. With this in mind William tried to sell off

the estate to the existing tenant farmers which was common practice at the time but in the end he had to auction the land off in lots. The house was sold to a consortium who stripped out its interiors and the lead off the roof just leaving the masonry and brick shell. Fortunately this early Georgian structure was saved before it could be demolished and is now in the hands of English Heritage. Its haunting shell can still be visited today.

Clough Hall, Kidsgrove, Staffordshire was a grand house and parkland which bordered the growing suburbs north of Stoke on Trent. After the First World War it was sold off and demolished in 1927. Part of the estate was bought up and developed for private housing with the name Clough Hall retained for the road and public house pictured here.

collections of artwork and valuables. Stanwick Hall in Yorkshire was one of five properties owned by the Dukes of Northumberland and after the 7th Duke died in 1918 the death duties forced the family to sell off this estate. Farms, cottages and land were sold off piecemeal before a number of rooms were professionally stripped out and sold to clients in Canada and the United States. One of these was bought by William Randolph Hearst, the newspaper magnet who was the inspiration for Orson Welles' character in *Citizen Kane*.

Many of those country estates close to expanding urban areas were snapped up by local authorities and private developers for new housing estates, especially around London where many suburban areas are still known by the old name of the mansions which stood there. The Capels had owned Cassiobury House for 400 years but it was sold after the 7th Earl was killed by a taxi in 1916. After the mansion was demolished in 1927 it became part of the urban expansion of Watford with an area of the estate becoming Cassiobury Park. Ford Hall, Sunderland, the home of General Havelock who helped quell the Indian Mutiny in 1857, was sold in 1924 to Sunderland Borough Council for a new housing estate which still bears its name. Some

country houses became schools, hotels or private institutions. Enham House, near Andover in Hampshire was purchased in 1918 by a group of businessmen who converted it into a centre for the rehabilitation of disabled servicemen returning from the war.

Not every country house estate was sold up reluctantly to pay tax bills. Philip Napier Miles owned the Kings Weston estate near Bristol and had already donated land from it before in 1919 he agreed to sell off over 200 acres at a low price to the city corporation. He was interested in the garden suburb movement and placed a covenant upon the land that it should only be used as a garden suburb with a housing density of no more than 12 houses per acre. He also retained the right for him and his architect to be consulted over the plans for what was to become the Sea Mills Estate. The houses were carefully arranged along the roads which radiated from or revolved around the central green area so that they allowed the maximum amount of light in and created carefully planned vistas. To avoid monotony short rows were stepped back and houses at road junctions set at an angle so they formed small squares along the roads. Large gardens and open spaces were also featured at the rear of houses and trees planted along the streets so that greenery could be seen out of all the windows. These planning ideas devised by architects like Richard Unwin before the war were to influence most other housing estates built during the Inter War years.

Sometimes families were unable to sell the country house and it was more economic to demolish it to avoid the expense of upkeep and paying probate. Hamilton Palace, Lanarkshire was one of the grandest houses in the country and was lent to the Navy for use as a hospital during the war. Upon its return to the 13th Duke of Hamilton in 1919 it was found to be in a poor state of repair through its wartime use and subsidence from the coal mines which had formerly brought money into the estate. The duke moved to one of his smaller

Hamilton Palace, Lanarkshire, Scotland was one of the grandest houses in the country and home to the Dukes of Hamilton for over 200 years. Yet this magnificent structure was stripped out and demolished after the war and the family moved into a smaller property they owned at Dungavel. It was here that Rudolf Hess, Hitler's long time associate, had intended to meet the Duke of Hamilton on his ill fated peace mission in 1941. He crashed his plane about 12 miles away from the Hamilton's house and spent the rest of his life a prisoner.

properties and this great Palladian mansion was demolished. Hooton Hall in Cheshire had been used by the Army during the war for training US and Canadian pilots, with the racecourse on the estate serving as a runway. As the military wanted to retain the estate the house, already in a poor state, was relatively worthless and was demolished in 1932. Part of the building was reused at Port Merion and the estate is now the site of the Ellesmere Port Vauxhall factory. Lord Anglesey found that the heavy taxation introduced in 1919 forced him to sell his Staffordshire estate of Beaudesert Hall and after he failed to find a buyer it was slowly stripped and the house largely demolished, although fragments remain as the demolition contractors went bust before they finished the job.

The Middle Classes

While the working masses struggled with unemployment and the gentry with taxation, the social group between began to prosper. The doctors, lawyers, teachers, shop owners, and businessmen who were the backbone of this middle class had only constituted around 5% of the population at the turn of the 20th century. These families shared the burden of loss at the end of the war but the sons who returned to their comfortable family homes in the new suburbs faced a more prosperous future. New light industries, a growth of clerical and managerial positions and the need for trained professionals to replace those who had died in the war created opportunities for educated men and women despite the economic gloom. This was especially the experience in the Midlands and

For many the inter war years presented new opportunities. The middle classes could afford a seaside holiday and some could even buy a home by the coast, preferably away from the crowds of day trippers. In 1934 a large estate was bought in the seaside town of Frinton on Sea, Essex by the South Coast Property Investment Co. New housing of mixed styles was planned aimed specifically at the middle classes, with a group of daring modern style houses closest to the beach. These bold designs which allowed sunlight to flood in, a key feature of inter war houses, proved hard to sell with flat roofs and only around forty were built.

The Neo Georgian style (top) had been fashionable for middle class housing in the early 1920s but once it had been adopted by local authorities for council estates it quickly fell from favour in the private sector. Most buyers from the late 1920s preferred Mock Tudor (bottom). Fake timber framing on the gables, patterned glass in the windows and traditional hanging tiles on the walls gave them reassurance that their investment was built to last.

South East where the population was growing and new companies were being established.

The most visible sign of this growth in the middle classes was in the building of private homes which were increasingly purchased with a mortgage rather than rented. Those with a steady income could find that, with falling prices, they were better off than before. Local building societies gained a huge increase in investment due to changes in tax policy and from the late 1920s were making mortgages more accessible and encouraging families to borrow money for a new home. This fuelled a boom in private house building during the 1930s as stout semi detached houses with curved bay windows, hipped roofs, and colourful glazing were erected along tree lined avenues and crescents. For many soldiers who returned from the western front and found employment within these new industries the inter-war years offered opportunities their parents never had. The potent image of a private family home nestling amongst trees out in the suburbs was very appealing and in stark contrast to the horrors they had endured during the war.

Private houses had to distinguish themselves from the new council houses being erected at the time. One way they did his was to face the front with a better quality brick than that used down the sides. Most council houses used cheap bricks with patchy finishes on all walls. A curved bay window at the front was a prominent sign that this was a better class of house with the upper sections of its casement windows filled with glass patterns. An arched porch with a recessed door and a window to the side illuminating the spacious hallway behind was also important. The size of many private houses though may not have been much bigger than those erected by local authorities and savings were made in both by lowering the height of ceilings which was possible now that cleaner electric lighting and gas heating was beginning to replace coal.

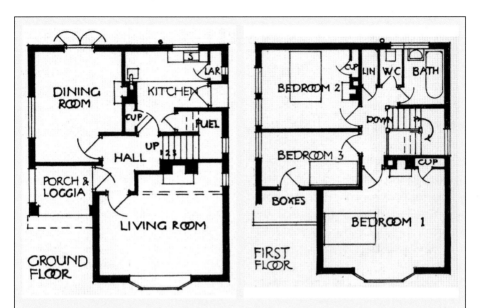

The new semi detached houses built for the middle classes were different in form from most houses built before the war. Rather than being set in tightly packed terraces these new homes on cheaper suburban land were more spacious, square and stout. Live in servants were now rare so there was no need for attics or basements and the scullery and stores which were formerly in a rear extension were now incorporated within the structure. They had a wide porch and hall, bay windows lighting the front living room and a kitchen for cooking and washing. The bathroom and toilet upstairs with running hot and cold water was a real luxury. In total nearly 3 million private homes were built in Britain during the inter war years, a large proportion in this form as illustrated in these contemporary plans by Edwin Gunn.

War Looms Again
1930–1939

The Great Depression

Britain's economy had largely stagnated during the 1920s. Any glimmers of a revival after the post war slump had been countered by the effects of the return to the Gold Standard which had increased the price of exports. Elsewhere around the world there had been more positive economic growth, even in Germany which was saddled with reparation payments from the First World War. In the United States the Roaring Twenties were boom years built upon easy credit and high consumer spending. An increasing number of people began speculating on financial markets, often taking out loans to buy more stocks. This came crashing down when prices began falling in the US during September and October 1929 and panic ensued as loans could not be paid back, money was withdrawn and banks failed. The effects of this Wall Street Crash rippled around the world and international trade suddenly started to fall. Countries began cutting back on spending and raising tariffs and barriers to trade and turned what could have been a short term crash into the Great Depression, the effects of which were felt by many people throughout the 1930s.

In Britain the rapid decline in world trade resulted in a sharp rise in unemployment during 1930. The Labour government under Ramsey MacDonald which had come to power in the previous year took a traditionally cautious approach but by August 1931 were forced into more drastic action. When they

Despite the economic slump new factories for the electrical, car, chemical and other light industries were built, mainly in the Midlands and South East. The iconic Art Deco Hoover Building, shown here, was built in 1933 in Perivale, West London along the new Western Avenue which opened the following year. In the areas along this new arterial expressway housing estates quickly sprang up, nearly all built by speculative builders for private ownership.

proposed reducing unemployment benefits the cabinet split and the government resigned. A new National Government was formed with MacDonald remaining as Prime Minister. They made immediate budget cuts and abandoned the Gold Standard, a move which caused the pound to drop in value by around 25%, making British exports cheaper. This helped reignite the economy and draw the country out of the economic crisis.

The effects of the Great Depression were very dependent upon where you lived. Those regions which relied upon industries like coal, shipbuilding, textiles and metal production and had seen little investment during the previous decade suddenly found themselves in an even worse situation. With the drop in world trade the demand for new ships fell by around 90% over the three years up to 1932, resulting in the closure of shipyards. In autumn 1936 the failure of Palmer's Shipyard in the North Eastern town of Jarrow inspired around 200 men and their female MP to march to London to highlight the suffering in their community.

Just as the Jarrow March showed the extreme lengths those who were blighted by unemployment were forced to go to, their route took them through areas of the Midlands

Charles Jenkinson, the driving force behind the mass clearance of slums in Leeds, was born in London in 1887. The son of a docker, he left school at 14 and went into bookkeeping whilst playing an active part in the local church and Labour Party. He was a conscientious objector when the war broke out but still served in the Royal Army Medical Corps while studying for Greek and Latin and eventually passing a law degree at Cambridge. In 1923 he was ordained a curate in Barking but after asking for a more challenging role he was appointed the vicar of Holbeck in Leeds, a notoriously run down area. After being elected a Labour councillor in 1930 he used his dual role and zealous character to fight for the clearance of the slums his congregation had to endure and upon becoming chair of the Housing Committee three years later could finally put his ideas into action.

and South East where the Great Depression had passed by with little negative effect. In the wake of leaving the Gold Standard interest rates were cut to 2% so loans and mortgages became affordable to many families who were employed in the light industries centred in these areas. This resulted in a boom in private house building which helped boost related trades, especially the electrical industry with the supply of fittings and appliances to these new homes. Of the new factories built in Britain in the years immediately after 1932 nearly 50% were erected

For women the inter-war years were a time of notable if slow change. There had been legislation immediately after the war which was seen as a reward for women for their contribution during the conflict. The right to vote was granted for women aged 30 and over in 1918 and this limit was lowered to 21 in 1928. The Sex Disqualification Act 1919 helped women go to university and get professional jobs and the Education Act 1918 had raised school leaving age to 14 and meant all girls could get a good education. Despite these steps forward the benefits were patchy and by the 1930s most women still found themselves restricted in their ambitions. New industries and the expanding civil service presented jobs which were regarded as suitable for women. Most were either office based clerical jobs like a typist or telephonist or were assembly jobs on the factory floor of new light industries. There was little opportunity for promotion, the shifts were long and pay low compared to male counterparts. In fact although women had received wages similar to men at the end of the war, by 1930 they were usually back to where they were before, generally around half the pay of men.

More restrictive still was the marriage bar which the civil service and other industries used to force women to leave work when they tied the knot. If they did not leave employment at this point they were certainly expected to as soon as they had children. Most authorities and even trade unions gave priority to preserving jobs for men especially when unemployment began to escalate from 1930. If women did lose their jobs then they would not receive the same support as men. After the war the government had been concerned with shortages of domestic servants and were keen to keep as many jobs as possible open for the returning soldiers so had restricted benefits to those women who were willing to return to their traditional roles. Even those who were eligible to receive it only got a reduced rate compared to male counterparts. Despite these barriers the number of women working rose and some broke into specialist and skilled roles. By the mid 1930s just over 30% of women were in employment and despite the restrictions of the marriage bar around 10% of married women also had a job.

The majority of women still worked at home, where the inter war years presented mixed experiences. Some found themselves struggling to cope with looking after war-wounded family members. Many had to deal with the stress of not only caring for an injured soldier on top of their domestic duties but also having to find other employment to bolster their reduced income. For most looking after the home was an arduous task. Washing clothes and sheets was still done by hand, carpet pieces and rugs had to be beaten outside, preparing and cooking food was time consuming and with coal fires all surfaces in the home needed regular cleaning. By the 1930s though many found themselves in new council houses or privately owned semis which promised, although did not always deliver, a reduced workload. New washing machines and vacuum cleaners for middle class homes were a benefit, a gas or electric cooker was easier to control than an old range, and new forms of heating reduced the need for dirty gas lighting and coal fires.

in London alone. It was around these new industries in the South East and Midlands that the bulk of private housing was built, creating vast suburbs which transformed the character of many towns and cities.

The Greenwood Act 1930

Although the Wheatley Act provided subsidies for the building of large numbers of council houses in the suburbs little progress had been made in clearing inner city slums. In some areas, despite the number of properties built in the 1920s, the shortage of housing actually grew and overcrowding remained an issue. The Minister of Health, Arthur Greenwood, in the new Labour government outlined in 1930 new legislation which was planned to finally tackle the problem. It would switch the focus from providing Homes fit for Heroes wherever they lived to specifically clearing the slums. He declared to the nation that 'those of us who are comfortably housed have a grave responsibility towards those who are not … large numbers of our fellow citizens and their children are living amongst surroundings which are a disgrace to our civilization'. Greenwood asked those listening to his broadcast to 'insist that the slums must go'.

The new act would encourage local authorities to clear the overcrowded back to backs and narrow courts of old unsanitary terraced housing and provide new homes for those who were displaced. The subsidies provided were crucially granted for the number of people displaced rather than just the number of houses demolished. Part of the reason for the lack of slum clearance under previous acts was that if there were 10 old houses but with 20 families crammed inside then the money would only be granted for another 10 properties and not the 20 which would be required; this act put that right. There were increased subsidies for councils where the price of

The demand for materials for new houses benefited many who worked in the brick industry. The London Brick Company expanded its operation in Bedfordshire where organic material in the local clay meant it could be fired in kilns without the need for coal, making it cheaper to produce. The company built a workers' village around their works during the late 1920s and 1930s with spacious housing as pictured here. They named this new community Stewartby after the family who were the directors of the company.

Arthur Greenwood, the son of a painter and decorator from Leeds, will probably be best remembered for the moment in September 1939 when as Labour's deputy leader he accused the Prime Minister, Neville Chamberlain, of wavering over what action to take after Germany had invaded Poland. 'Britain and all that Britain stands for are in peril,' he stated in his speech and the very next day Britain declared war on Germany. He was also key in supporting Churchill's rejection of a German peace offer in the following May when the war cabinet were in two minds as to whether to accept it. It was ten years earlier however that Greenwood had made a lasting contribution to help some of those who had fought in the earlier war escape from unsanitary and cramped old terraces. As Minister of Health in Ramsey MacDonald's Labour government he introduced the Housing Act 1930 which was the first that was effective in starting the large scale clearance of the slums.

land was unusually high and space limited, as was the case in London. In these situations blocks of flats were going to be the most effective form of accommodation. These had already been built successfully in Liverpool and were used as models for new schemes elsewhere. It also gave councils permission to offer tenants rebates so that the rent would not be beyond what the displaced families could realistically afford. The act tackled some of the key issues which had prevented earlier attempts to clear the slums from working and the Greenwood Act, as it would be known, would see the first mass clearance of these blighted areas. The dire financial situation of the early 1930s meant that most schemes did not get under way until around 1933 but over the following years hundreds of thousands of houses and flats were erected for displaced families. The 1935 Housing Act provided further powers and initiatives to reduce overcrowding, rebuild existing housing and to erect new homes for those evicted.

Housing (Financial Provisions) Act 1933

Aside from the need to clear the slums, there was still government money being spent on developing council housing estates to reduce the general shortage of houses. With the dire financial state the National Government found itself in during 1932 there was a need to reduce spending further and the removal of loans and subsidies for this housing was a key target. It was costing vastly more than those who had introduced the first 'Homes Fit For Heroes' legislation back in 1919 had envisaged, and the public finances were not in the Exchequer's opinion able to sustain such a policy. The public mood had changed from those optimistic years immediately after the war and would be more tolerant of a change of policy. Opposition from Labour had also been removed as they had been heavily defeated in the election in the previous year. The intention was now to empower the private sector so they could provide cheap housing for rent. The government worked with the building societies to put the legislation in place as they were best positioned to provide the finance, being among the few institutions with available funds at the time. The aim was that they would supply the money for private builders to develop cheap new housing, with the funds they were lending guaranteed in part by the local councils and Ministry of Health. The local authority would work closely with building societies and approve the plans before the development could take place. The act when passed also ended the

subsidies laid down in the 1924 Wheatley Act.

A similar provision had been made in the Chamberlain Act of 1923 which had resulted in very few buildings being erected, and this act was equally disappointing. Just over 20,000 houses were built under the 1933 act

Slum conditions
This picture of a family living in slum conditions might seem from the Victorian age but it dates from the 1930s. At this time people living in these old cramped terraces still did not have basic sanitation and shared communal toilets with neighbours. In back to backs the situation was even worse. Most domestic activities took place in the living room including the birth of a child and laying out of a deceased family member. Bath night was performed in a tin tub on the floor with hot water boiled in the kettle on the small range which provided the only heat in the house. Without adequate space inside and no yard at the rear, it made it hard to upgrade these unsanitary homes.

> **The Great Depression** was the worst economic crisis of the 20th century with gross domestic production falling to lower levels than in any other recession since. The number of registered unemployed rose from around one million to well over three million at the worst point in 1932, a rise from 10% to around 22% of the working population. Many others who were not registered only worked part time or had falling incomes from wage cuts and reduced hours. In areas reliant upon the old heavy industries unemployment rose to record levels, in some places accounting for up to 70% of the workforce. Benefits were restricted initially and ran out after 15 weeks so many families faced extreme hardship. New unemployment benefit introduced in 1931 was an improvement as it took into account the needs of the applicant. However it could only be received after inspectors had ensured that they did not have any hidden savings and these intrusive investigations were resented by many of those who were just trying to survive. The government also tried to create work by commissioning building projects from new roads to improving old canals but these were never on a large enough scale to make a significant difference. Even with help from charitable soup kitchens which were provided in many cities it was found that around a quarter of all families were surviving upon a subsistence diet, with signs of malnutrition amongst their children.

out of the approximately 300,000 houses constructed annually in the mid 1930s. Part of the blame for its failure fell on the local authorities, many of whom now saw themselves as housing providers and were often unwilling to cooperate with the building societies or were slow to approve plans. Building societies also found the deal less attractive than they had hoped and most pumped their money into the private housing market which was rapidly expanding at the time.

Slum Clearance

Leeds had a notorious problem with back to back houses which were still being built in the early 20th century. Although most of those later types had the basic sanitary requirements there were still thousands living in smaller, older houses around cramped courtyards or along narrow rows. There were over 75,000 of them still occupied at the end of the war with around a fifth having only two rooms. By 1930 Leeds Council had erected nearly 10,000 new council houses but this had little effect on the slum areas of the city as the rent for these new spacious suburban homes was around double that charged for a back to back and beyond the purse of the poorly paid. It took the Christian socialist vicar and Labour councillor, Charles Jenkinson, who had become chairman of the council housing committee in 1933 to try and solve the problem. He introduced a system of differential rents so that new tenants paid what they could afford towards the rent of a new council house and a

The speed with which the slums needed to be cleared in Leeds meant that flats would have to be provided. These could be erected on the cleared sites close to the city centre which would also solve the problem of the difficult commute and dislocated feeling many of those moving to suburban estates complained of. Representatives from the council made a visit to the Karl-Marx-Hof in Vienna, a modern block of flats completed in 1930 which surrounded green spaces and communal facilities. In the Austrian capital the authorities had decided not to extend the suburbs but instead rebuild the inner city area with a series of 'Hofs' (courts).

This inspired the planners from Leeds to design a similar set of multi-storey flats at Quarry Hill, with nearly 1,000 apartments enclosed within an outer ring forming a fortress-like exterior with huge arched openings to access the centre. They would be built using a steel frame and concrete sections prefabricated on site which could be erected quickly and without the need for expensive skilled bricklayers. Not only would tenants have a scullery, bathroom, toilet and electric lighting in each flat which would be accessed by lifts (rare at this date) but they would also have facilities like a bus station, swimming pools, shops, a nursery and a large communal hall. Despite the ambition, the method of construction was fraught with problems, delaying completion and the cost of ongoing repairs meant that most of the planned facilities were never built. The Quarry Hill flats were demolished only 40 years later.

rebate covered the shortfall. The homes they were given would also now be judged on the family's need rather than their ability to pay so in effect a slum dweller with a large family could occupy a three bedroom council house and pay less than his neighbour in a smaller property. This system inevitably caused conflict between neighbours, with rent strikes from those who now had to pay more and the scheme's unpopularity meant that Jenkinson lost his seat only three years later. However in this brief

Jenkinson's housing committee in Leeds erected new estates and expanded existing ones including Middleton, Belle Isle, Gipton, Halton and Seacroft. Schools, shops and churches like the Church of the Epiphany, Gipton, pictured here, were provided in these areas. His own congregation in the slum area of Holbeck were uprooted and moved to Belle Isle and a new church for them erected there. However some of the existing tenants, many of whom found their rent increased to subsidise those on lower incomes, resented these new families, claiming they lowered the standards of the estate.

period the worst back to back houses had been demolished and most of the families who lived there moved into the 9,000 new homes the council built between 1933 and 1937.

The 1930 Housing Act demanded that local authorities had to present plans for the clearing of slum areas and the building of new housing for the evicted families. In Bristol this resulted in the building of new, or the extending of existing, estates to accommodate those evicted by slum clearances. The new houses on the whole still featured front and rear gardens, a separate bathroom and two or three bedrooms but now the houses were more compact, often set in rows rather than being semi-detached and were more tightly fitted in along the roads and avenues. The largest of these was Filwood Park, a westerly extension of the Knowle

The Knowle estate in Bristol had developed in phases. The original spacious 'Homes fit for Heroes' houses built along Broad Walk were followed by another area of more compact housing to the south under the Wheatley Act. Then from 1930 a new section originally called Filwood Park but now known as Knowle West was developed with a higher density of housing but still retaining the gardens and green spaces which characterised inter war estates. A cinema was opened in 1938 within the estate but only on the condition that the poorest families would have to use a discreet entrance round the back, while the better class of customer could use the main foyer at the front!

In Poplar the London County Council erected a number of blocks of flats to rehouse slum dwellers. The largest of these were the Will Crooks and West Ferry Estates where over 400 individual flats in blocks five storeys high were built by 1939. Not everyone wanted to be moved into these bright new homes. Some complained that they did not want to lose their gardens or that they feared a loss of privacy, despite their existing homes being unsanitary. Shopkeepers were justified in objecting as they would lose the existing trade from nearby businesses when they were uprooted and moved to a new residential area.

estate which had been established to the south west of Bristol in 1919. It included a community centre, shops, churches and even its own cinema and by the end of the decade could boast a population of around 27,000 people.

In Poplar in East London, which the LCC identified as one of the areas in greatest need of slum clearance, the problem was the lack of available space. As with many places across the capital where land values were generally high the authorities turned to building four or five storey blocks of flats or rows of maisonettes rather than new housing estates to accommodate the evicted slum tenants. The process of identifying the areas to be cleared through to the final movement of families was usually a long drawn out affair. Firstly the process could not get under way until there was land available for replacement housing. Even after the local health officer had identified houses which could not economically be brought up to a standard fit for human habitation they would have to wait until the local authority had acquired a site where new flats could be built. There could be further delay caused by some residents whose businesses would be affected by being moved and private landowners whose property might need a compulsory purchase order placed upon it. In

While the LCC built a large number of flats in Poplar during the 1930s the local borough council made a notable contribution. Their structures seemed to have a bit more external flair with Art Deco styled balconies with streamlined curved ends as at Constant House in this picture. One of these blocks also included special flats for pensioners, a rare provision in municipal housing at this date.

some cases the process could be more straightforward if the slum area was suitable for the new flats. In this situation a number of families would have to be accommodated elsewhere in order for the first houses to be demolished and a new block built on that spot. When this first phase was complete then families from neighbouring properties could move in and another block be erected and so on until the site had been redeveloped. Even on relatively small sites this process could take three or four years to complete.

Rural Council Housing

For most of the 1920s and early 1930s the main focus of housing was to serve the urban population. Virtually nothing had been provided in rural districts as most authorities felt that agricultural workers were too poorly paid to be able to afford the rent. Even after the passing of the 1926 Housing for Rural Workers Act most councils preferred to subsidise landlords so they could update existing workers' cottages rather than build new homes. Those that were built were normally small in number and limited to sites in the centre of villages where unsanitary or dilapidated housing had been pulled down. It was not until the 1936 Housing Act that local authorities finally received funds to enable them to build a larger number of rural council houses. Most of these were built on new land on the edge of villages where spacious but plain semis and rows of houses are characteristic of this late 1930s development.

War looms again

By 1939 the building of houses and flats for the public and private sector had developed at such a rapid rate that around 30% of the entire housing stock of the country dated from the inter war years. Since 1924 when the Wheatley Act was passed and the private sector had recovered somewhat from the war, around 200,000 homes were built each

It was not until the 1930s that the issue of unsanitary housing in rural districts began to be tackled. Some early housing can be found within villages like this example from Suffolk, but most was built on the edge of the village and dates from the 1930s and post Second World War period.

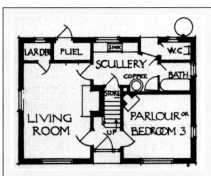

A plan of a rural cottage from Edwin Gunn's 1932 book *Economy in House Design*. It squeezes in the basic facilities with a range in the living room for cooking, a small scullery for washing, a separate bath and toilet and two bedrooms upstairs.

For many young couples and families modernist houses appealed as their bright walls, large windows and continental style flat roofs were exotic and made a welcome break from dreary old terraces. It was something new and exciting, a clean break from the First World War and economic gloom. Modernism also had the potential to provide spacious accommodation at a cheaper price using new materials and construction methods. Most inter war experiments in concrete and steel were limited to commercial buildings and a few exclusive houses. Some estates were built with stark white walls, streamlined curving bays and flat roofs although they were usually made from conventional brick rendered over to appear like the fashionable concrete. In our wet climate flat roofs proved unpopular and the style was too radical for most private buyers. This example in Leek, Staffs was built as one of a number of show houses for a new development but all the buyers opted for the traditional look of its neighbours and it remains the only one of its style built in the town.

year, peaking at over 350,000 in the mid 1930s. Of this new stock over 1 million homes had been built by local authorities and over 2½ million for the private sector. There had also been a notable shift in the way in which property was held. Before the war only around 10% of homes were privately owned, the other 90% being rented with barely 1% of these being council provided accommodation. However by 1939 this had shifted so that over 30% owned their own house and 70% rented, of whom over 10% were council tenants. Despite this boom in house building the lack of work

in the public sector before the war and the ever present shortage of homes meant that as the new decade approached there was still much to be done. The problem of the slums in particular was still ever present and despite over 200,000 families being moved into healthier accommodation during this period estimates at the time calculated that more than double this figure were still living in substandard housing.

The promise made by Lloyd George in 1918 of creating hundreds of thousands of Homes fit for Heroes may have fallen short of his ambitious

Just as the ambitious plans and generous dimensions of houses laid out in the Tudor Walters report had been progressively cut back to make new council housing more economic to build, so the speculative builder erecting semis for the middle classes in the 1930s could simplify the layout to save costs. A rectangular plan with no awkward rear extensions saved on materials and reduced the time it took to build. Also, limiting the number of internal walls to a bare minimum and fitting the toilet in the bathroom saved digging extra foundations and erecting walls, reducing costs further. The builder of private housing usually did not bother providing the numerous built-in cupboards which were a favourite feature of council provided accommodation. Freestanding furniture was cheaper and could be provided in most cases by the buyer.

targets. Many of the soldiers returning from the Western Front and workers who manufactured their arms and armaments would have been disappointed that home life did not improve upon their return home. Fluctuating economic fortunes, the failure of many of the old industries and high unemployment meant that many were soon in a worse situation than when they left in 1914. For those who in addition to these concerns suffered the scars and mental effects of the war there was a continuing struggle to come to terms with domestic life. However as the 1930s drew on so jobs in new factories and offices, and the increasing number of

affordable and healthy homes being made available, allowed many of those who had served their country to finally feel the benefits.

This progress was suddenly cut short in September 1939. In Germany, loans from the United States had helped fund reparation payments and rebuild the economy but with the Wall Street Crash these came to an end. The resulting financial crisis and effects of the global depression resulted in unemployment soaring to around 30% by 1932. The centralist German government failed to act with sufficient vigour and collapsed in the wake of political unrest

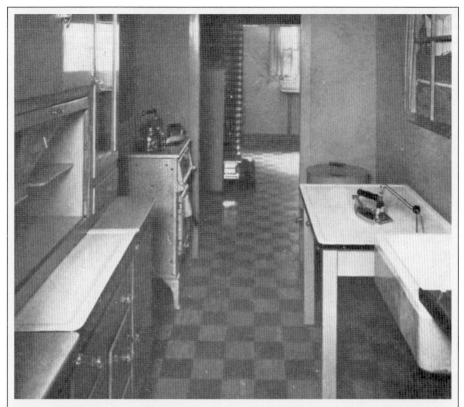

A thoroughly modern 1930s kitchen with the latest appliances and storage units. Most kitchens were originally short of space like this but old coal stores and larders have often been knocked out since to increase room.

instigated by extremist Communists and Nazis. Adolf Hitler, who had served in the German army during the war, came to power in the following year and his Nazi Party increased government spending on major building projects, which helped bring down unemployment. He had long resented Germany's treatment at Versailles and largely ignored the restriction made on his country's military strength in the treaty, instead pumping money into rebuilding the armed forces. Despite warnings from key politicians like Churchill, Britain was slow to respond to the threat and Neville Chamberlain, who had now become Prime Minister, appeased many doubters when he returned from Munich in 1938 declaring 'peace for our time'. Less than a year later he had to announce to the nation that Britain was once again at war with Germany.

Further Information

USEFUL WEBSITES

Finding out more about family members who served in the First World War and their life after the conflict is much easier now that many of the documents are available online. Unfortunately, many service records were destroyed during bombing in the Second World War (approximately 60%) so other sources, most notably the medal rolls and index cards which are virtually complete, are a valuable source of information. Before searching online or visiting The National Archives it is useful if you can find out as much about the soldier as possible, including full name and his address before he left on service. His regimental number, rank or unit he served in might be on old documents, personal letters or written on the back of a photo that are in your family's possession or are recorded on the rim or rear of old service medals. If you believe the soldier was killed during the war then start by checking the Commonwealth War Graves Commission website (www.cwgc. org). The following websites have further information about starting the search for a past relative and contain copies of relevant documents which can be viewed online (usually for a fee or subscription):

Family research:
www.nationalarchives.gov.uk/help-with-your-research/research-guides/british-army-soldiers-after-1913
www.thegreatwar.co.uk
www.ancestry.co.uk
www.findmypast.co.uk
www.forces-war-records.co.uk
www.longlongtrail.co.uk
www.pals.org.uk/research.htm
livesofthefirstworldwar.org/ww1-records
www.thegazette.co.uk/awards-and-accreditation/ww1
www.forces-war-records.co.uk
www.iwm.org.uk

Memorials:
www.cwgc.org
www.findagrave.com
www.ww1wargraves.co.uk
www.warmemorialsonline.org.uk
www.hellfirecorner.co.uk
www.warmemorials.org/
www.iwm.org.uk/corporate/projects-and-partnerships/war-memorials-register
www.thenma.org.uk/
ukwarmemorials.org
Livesofthefirstworldwar.org

Post war council housing:
municipaldreams.wordpress.com
fet.uwe.ac.uk/conweb/house_ages/council_housing
www.pre-war-housing.org.uk
socialhousinghistory.org.uk

Other useful sites:
www.worldwar1.com
www.firstworldwar.com
www.army.mod.uk/structure/32321.
aspx
encyclopedia.1914-1918-online.net
www.british-history.ac.uk
www.lostheritage.org.uk/lh_complete_
list.html
www.armymuseums.org.uk

PLACES TO VISIT
Imperial War Museum, Lambeth
Road, London SE1 6HZ, Tel: 020 7416
5000, www.iwm.org.uk/visits/iwm-
london
Imperial War Museum North,
Trafford Wharf Rd, Stretford,
Manchester M17 1TZ, Tel: 0161 836
4000, www.iwm.org.uk/visits/iwm-
north
National Army Museum, Royal
Hospital Road, Chelsea, London SW3
4HT, Tel: 020 7730 0717, www.nam.

ac.uk
The Devil's Porridge Museum,
Stanfield, Annan Road, Eastriggs,
Dumfries and Galloway, DG12 6TF,
Tel: 01461 700021,
www.devilsporridge.org.uk
The Black Country Living Museum,
Tipton Road, Dudley DY1 4SQ. Tel:
0121 557 9643, www.bclm.co.uk
Valence House (Becontree Council
Estate), Becontree Avenue, Dagenham,
RM8 3HT, Tel: 020 8227 2034 www.
lbbd.gov.uk/residents/leisure-libraries-
and-museums/valence-house
Tenement House (National Trust
Scotland), 145 Buccleuch Street,
Glasgow, G3 6QN, Tel: 0141 333 0183,
www.nts.org.uk/Visit/Tenement-House
Mr Straw's House (National
Trust), 5-7 Blyth Grove, Worksop,
Nottinghamshire, S81 0JG, Tel: 01909
482380, www.nationaltrust.org.uk/mr-
straws-house

BOOKS
First World War Army Service Records, William Spencer (The National Archives, 2008)
Council Housing and Culture: the history of a social experiment, Alison Ravetz, (Routledge, 2001)
Working-Class Cultures in Britain. Gender, Class and Ethnicity, Joanna Bourke (Routledge, 1994)
Borrowed Time: The Story of Britain between the Wars, Roy Hattersley (Little, Brown, 2007)
A Social History of Housing 1815-1985, John Burnett (Routledge, 1991)
The Thirties. An Intimate History, Juliet Gardiner (Harper Press, 2011)
War, Disability and Rehabilitation in Britain: 'Soul of a Nation', Julie Anderson (Manchester University Press, 2016)
Forgotten Lunatics of the Great War, Peter Barham (Yale University Press, 2004)
Broken Men: shell shock, treatment and recovery in Britain, 1914-1930, Fiona Reid (Continuum, 2011)

Glossary

Armistice: A truce or temporary agreement to cease warfare. The Armistice refers specifically to the document which ended the war on the Western Front and was signed at 11am on 11 November 1918.

Arts and Crafts: A style which centred on the revival of old crafts and the use of vernacular materials. Buildings were inspired by old farmhouses and cottages rather than grand houses.

Asbestos: A fire resistant boarding made from a fibrous silicate mineral used in houses throughout this period. Although safe when intact it can be very dangerous when broken and the fibres are inhaled.

Back to backs: Compact Victorian terraced houses which share side and rear walls so have no rear and often no front garden.

Bargeboard: Timber boards which protect the ends of the sloping roof on a gable end and were often decorated.

Bay window: A window projecting from the facade of a house, of varying height but always resting on the ground.

Blighty: Term used by English soldiers for home from Hindustani 'bilayati' meaning foreign land.

Bitumen: A petroleum derivative used for waterproofing flat roofs and forming a damp proof layer in walls or under floors.

Boche: Another name for a German probably from the French 'tete de boche' meaning obstinate person.

Bonding: The way bricks are laid in a wall with the different patterns formed by alternative arrangements of headers (the short ends) and stretchers (the long side).

Bully beef: Tinned corned beef, one of the staple rations of the British Army.

Casement window: A window which is hinged along one side.

Cavity walls: Walls formed from an inner and outer skin of the same or different materials with a thin gap between.

Chit: A slip or receipt from the Hindustani 'cittha' meaning a note.

Civvy: A civilian.

Colours, With The: Serving in the army. Often found on forms when referring to length of service.

Conscription: The compulsory enlistment of people into military service.

Corps: A military unit usually comprising of a number of divisions.

Crittall windows: Metal framed windows made by the Essex based company Crittall.

Damp proof course: A waterproof barrier incorporated within walls just above ground level. In this period liquid or sheet bitumen was widely used.

Demob/Demobilisation: The process of standing down a country's armed forces at the end of a conflict and returning soldiers and support staff to civilian life.

Eaves: The section of the roof timbers under the tiles or slates where they meet the wall, usually protected by a fascia board.

Facade: The main vertical face of the house.

Flue: The duct for smoke from the fireplace up into the chimney.

Fritz: Another name for a German, which came from the popular name Friedrich.

Funk: Someone who was in a state of fear, nervousness, or depression.

Gable: The pointed upper section of wall at the end of a pitched roof.

Go west: To be killed.

Hipped roof: A roof with a slope on all four sides.

Hun: After the Kaiser urged his troops to behave like Attilla's Huns in order to strike fear into the enemy this became a nickname for the Germans.

Jakes: An old name for toilets or latrines.

Jerry: Another term for a German which was popular later in the war.

Joists: Timber, concrete or steel beams which support the floor.

Lintel: A flat beam which is fitted above a door or window to take the load of the wall above.

Moulding: A decorative strip of wood, stone or plaster.

Mufti: A term for civilian clothes from the Arabic for 'free'.

Pandemic: An outbreak of disease which is prevalent over a whole country or the world.

Parapet: The top section of wall which continues above the sloping end of the roof.

Pitch: The angle by which a roof slopes. A plain sloping roof of two sides is called a pitched roof.

Purlins: Large timbers which run the length of the roof supporting the rafters.

Pushing up daisies: Dead and buried.

Rafters: Timbers which form the slope of the roof with laths running across their upper surface onto which the roof covering is fixed.

Render: A protective covering for a wall made from two or three layers of cement.

Scullery: A wet room specifically used for washing clothes, pots and utensils.

Semis: A semi detached house. Two separate homes side by side in a single unit under one roof.

Shell: A hollow metal pointed case which contained an explosive and was fired from guns and howitzers.

Shrapnel: Metal balls ejected from a shell of the same name used to take out men and horses on the battlefield and named after its inventor, General H. Shrapnel. Often used to describe any metal fragments from other types of shell.

Spalling: The flaking away of pieces of surface material usually when steel in reinforced concrete rusts and expands.

Streamlined: The shaping of cars, planes and trains to make them more aerodynamic and mirrored on buildings in the 1930s for stylistic reasons.

Ticket: An official discharge from the army often for medical reasons.

Tommy: The name for a British soldier, from the name Tommy Atkins which was used on specimen forms.

Vernacular: Buildings made from local materials in styles and method of construction passed down within a distinct area, as opposed to architect-designed structures made from mass produced materials.

Western Front: The battlefront through Belgium and France which marked the line between Allied and German forces.

Index

OTHER TITLES FROM COUNTRYSIDE BOOKS

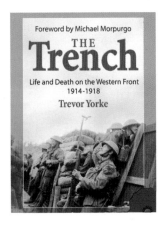

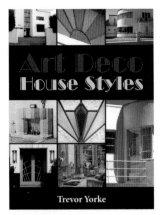

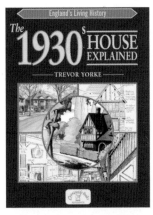

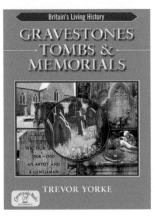

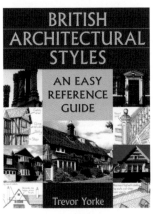

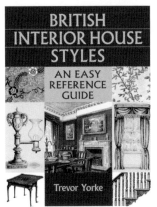

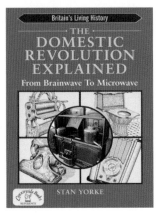

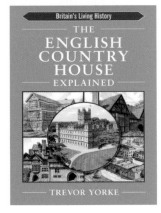

To see our full range of books please visit
www.countrysidebooks.co.uk

Follow us on @ CountrysideBooks